Get Out of Your Own Way at Work . . .

and Help Others Do the Same

Get Out of Your Own Way at Work...

and Help Others Do the Same

Conquer Self-Defeating Behavior on the Job

MARK GOULSTON, M.D.

A PERIGEE BOOK

A PERIGEE BOOK
Published by the Penguin Group
Penguin Group (USA) Inc.
375 Hudson Street, New York, New York 10014, USA
Penguin Group (Canada), 90 Eglinton Avenue East, Suite 700, Toronto, Ontario M4P 2Y3, Canada
(a division of Pearson Penguin Canada Inc.)
Penguin Books Ltd., 80 Strand, London WC2R 0RL, England
Penguin Ireland, 25 St. Stephen's Green, Dublin 2, Ireland (a division of Penguin Books Ltd.)
Penguin Group (Australia), 250 Camberwell Road, Camberwell, Victoria 3124, Australia
(a division of Pearson Australia Group Pty. Ltd.)
Penguin Books India Pvt. Ltd., 11 Community Centre, Panchsheel Park, New Delhi—110 017, India
Penguin Group (NZ), Cnr. Airborne and Rosedale Roads, Albany, Auckland 1310, New Zealand
(a division of Pearson New Zealand Ltd.)
Penguin Books (South Africa) (Pty.) Ltd., 24 Sturdee Avenue, Rosebank, Johannesburg 2196, South Africa

Penguin Books Ltd., Registered Offices: 80 Strand, London WC2R 0RL, England

While the author has made every effort to provide accurate telephone numbers and Internet addresses at
the time of publication, neither the publisher nor the author assumes any responsibility for errors, or for
changes that occur after publication. Further, the publisher does not have any control over and does not
assume any responsibility for author or third-party websites or their content.

PRINTING HISTORY
G. P. Putnam's Sons hardcover edition / October 2005
Perigee trade paperback edition / October 2006

Perigee trade paperback ISBN: 0-399-53285-4

The Library of Congress has cataloged the G. P. Putnam's Sons hardcover edition as follows:

Goulston, Mark.
    Get out of your own way at work . . . and help others do the same: conquer self-defeating behavior on
      the job / Mark Goulston.
        p.   cm.
    ISBN 0-399-15266-0
1. Work—Psychological aspects.   2. Self-defeating behavior.   3. Self-management (Psychology).
4. Success—Psychological aspects.   5. Organizational behavior.   I. Title.
HF5548.8.G668   2005   2005046576
158.1—dc22

PRINTED IN THE UNITED STATES OF AMERICA

10   9   8   7   6   5   4   3   2

Most Perigee Books are available at special quantity discounts for bulk purchases for sales promotions, pre-
miums, fund-raising, or educational use. Special books, or book excerpts, can also be created to fit specific
needs. For details, write: Special Markets, The Berkley Publishing Group, 375 Hudson Street, New York,
New York 10014.

To the memories of
Albert A. Dorskind and Ken Florence,
my mentors and friends,
this book is gratefully dedicated.

Contents

Introduction

Potential Is a Terrible Thing to Waste

> Everybody here has the ability to do anything I do and much beyond. Some of you will and some of you won't. For those who won't, it will be because you *get in your own way*, not because the world doesn't allow you.
>
> —Warren Buffett (speaking at the University of Washington)

YOU OR YOUR PEOPLE have the talent, education, and skills to do much more than you are currently doing. So what's getting in your way? If it's people you work with, what's getting in their way?

After my first book, *Get Out of Your Own Way*, was

published, I received hundreds of letters from people whose self-defeating behavior had caused them to be unhappy not just in their personal lives but also in their professional lives. Many of these readers had lost out on pay increases, promotions, and advancement. My clinical practice suddenly filled with men and women who, for a variety of reasons of their own making, had put their reputations, jobs, and careers in jeopardy.

One such patient was John. Fifty-five years old and prematurely gray, John was clearly suffering. Worry lines had plowed deeply into his forehead, and he walked with a slump of disappointment. The previous week, John had been fired from his job as an accountant because he refused to adapt to inevitable change. The challenge had been to learn a complex new software platform on which the company had bet its future. Resenting the "adapt or die" requirement, John ignored the hints, suggestions, warnings, and the ultimatum. Instead he led a rebellion—trying to convince people in his department that the company was better off staying with the old system. And so he was fired, after devoting fifteen years of his life to the firm.

Racked with self-doubt and disappointment, John was also frightened. He was very worried about the welfare of his family. Most of all he was angry. Rather than confronting the unrealistic fear that he couldn't learn a new program, John lost his job. Rather than open up, he closed down. John's career at the firm should have been long and proud, with a gold watch, a retirement party, and a fat 401K to greet him at the end. But he lost all this because he couldn't get out of his own way. John's self-defeating behavior overran him. He was a man alone and scared.

Now, I'm not a Jack Welch–style boss. I'm not an investigative reporter. I'm a doctor—a healer, a listener, a helper—who works with self-sabotagers or the bosses who must manage them. My job is to help my clients recognize and overcome their obstacles and become better and more successful—or help them to help others do the same—because I believe potential is a terrible thing to waste.

You may feel like you just need a little tweaking to reach your pinnacle. But more likely you feel a bit like John—somewhat alone and scared. You may have hit a wall at your own company, or at least had a close enough call to send you to this book. You might wake up at two-thirty A.M. worrying about that last meeting with the boss, or obsessing over that last cryptic dialogue with a colleague or a direct report.

Or perhaps you're thinking of some of your people who squander their potential as the window of opportunity for terrific careers closes more on them each day.

The strong response from working people to *Get Out of Your Own Way* caused me to extend my clinical practice to consulting in the business world. For the past several years, I've worked with companies ranging from family businesses to Fortune 100 corporate giants. I've worked with aggressive CEOs, impulsive senior vice presidents, pushy salespeople, depressed customer service representatives, and hundreds of others. All of these people had an ax to grind, or nursed a deep, abiding fear that either held them back or drove them to act out in inappropriate ways. All deserved to be more successful. And this is important: In most cases and despite their obvious problems, *all of their companies believed in them and were willing to give them at least one more chance.* That was why they had hired me to help.

I've spent hundreds of hours talking with people who are on the verge of committing hara-kiri at work. In almost every case, they have hardly a clue of what is "happening" to them. Any real awareness of their own role in the catastrophe that has happened, or is about to happen, is in short supply. Blame is their curtain for fear.

Consider:

- the sales executive who measures his self-worth by his commission, and bitterly resents his boss for continually raising the bar to discouraging heights and who then proceeds to take out his frustration on his family or his health;

- the operations manager who boasts about his personal accomplishments in a company meeting while his hardworking team watches and steams;

- the Ivy League financial analyst resentfully picking up the slack of his "incompetent" colleagues;

- the CEO who gets a secret thrill from slamming a sweaty palm on the conference table and seeing the blood drain from his underlings' faces;

- the marketing specialist who thinks it's okay to pad the expense report just a little;

- the administrative assistant who shows up late four days in a row and wonders why people aren't helping her out;

- the colleague who asks intrusive questions about the "tenth floor"—and the tenth-floor manager who asks about her;

- the woman who's so angry at the offhand remark from her boss that she misses a critical deadline.

If all of this conniving and paranoia sounds like a Dilbert cartoon, it is—and yet Dilbert is real-world stuff. Because the corporate life, as we know it, is dreadfully dysfunctional in many ways, it's easy to blame.

There's the impersonality of technology, of hierarchy, of politics, of patriarchy, of short-term thinking, of hypocrisy, of the lack or insincerity of communication, and on and on. This is not to say that the corporate system does not need massive correction, or that too many corporations are blind to the needs of even the most senior of their employees. But I would argue that, despite the massive betrayals at Enron et al., the majority of companies (and their leaders) aren't blinded by the systemic corporate mind-set. Business books and magazines are full of helpful prescriptions for you who must navigate the system on your own.

On a day-to-day level, your social contract with your company goes something like this: *I'll give you my time, energy, brainpower, and the sweat of my brow. In exchange, you give me a salary and (if I'm lucky) health insurance and other benefits.* Sounds simple. What is not overtly expressed in this equation—and shows up during the performance review process—is that *you are your work.* As such, you expect your work to confer upon you general approval, recognition, financial and social success, and happiness.

No, it's *never* just about collecting a paycheck. It is about self-esteem. And a company can't confer that on you. Earning self-esteem—and its twin sister, success—is *your* job.

Why We Get in Our Own Way

It's painfully obvious what self-defeating behavior is. A quick perusal of the table of contents of this book will make it immediately clear. Without even knowing the contents, however, few people would doubt that the behaviors identified in these pages are self-defeating.

The truth is that most of us, regardless of what we say, experience the workplace as a family. The subconscious equation: boss as parent, or colleague as sibling. Most psychologists will tell you that unresolved issues with our biological families will spill over into the workplace.

But I'd go further. The workplace is really a schoolyard. Maybe gym clothes have been replaced by business attire (although gym clothes *are* the business attire at more than a few companies), but it's astounding how the rivalries, backbiting, gossip, cliques, attitudes, and behaviors formed in the schoolyard of your childhood continue in your adult career.

I suspect that one of the reasons the ideas expressed here resonate with working people is that self-defeating behavior is so deeply embarrassing to them. It's one thing to sabotage a relationship with an individual friend or lover. It's quite another to self-immolate in the public realm of the office, which serves as a magnifying glass for personal issues. Do something dumb at home, and only your family notices. Do something stupid at work, and it's enlarged a hundredfold by a gossiping department or, in the worst cases, a million readers of *The Wall Street Journal*.

The question is: Where does self-defeating behavior come from?

Since the publication of *Get Out of Your Own Way*, I have discovered more and more parallels between my work as a physician, clinician, and scientist and the world of business.

I have become re-enthused about the science of human embryology. The development of the human fetus follows evolution up the phylogenetic tree of the animal kingdom: A human fetus, early on, resembles a sponge, a worm, and a fish. In the past few years, I've been fascinated by the embryology of the human brain. It grows from a few neural cells, to a neural tube, to the formation of ventricles and the cerebral cortex. What start out as nerve cells that react by simple reflexes end up as complex, highly evolved (and wonderfully named) "executive functions" that do all the things we need at work, like commanding the way we make decisions, communicating with others, and coming up with creative solutions to problems.

It turns out that self-defeating behavior is closer to our reflexive, early-neural, unthinking, animal nature than to our higher human, thoughtful nature. Individuals with self-defeating habits who find themselves in the corporate system typically display one of two types of animal responses, which I liken to those of nervous show dogs in the ring.

One type of show dog growls when it's afraid ("fearful aggression"). Another dog cowers and backs away ("fearful avoidance"). Both are instinctive behaviors that, unless trained out of them, automatically banish even the most well bred of show dogs from the ring and out of competition. And both are flip sides of the same coin of fear.

Animals are not the only living creatures to manifest fear in ways that are self-defeating. In the human animal, overt and covert displays of avoidance and aggression in the workplace are dangerous stuff. They sabotage the displayer. The price is nothing less than success and happiness, not to mention sacrificing a shot at winning "Best in Show."

Most people who self-sabotage in response to fear are in denial. They don't begin to fathom the extent to which their animal responses steal from their present and future. Instead of looking squarely at what they themselves might have done to bring on their trouble, self-saboteurs might take comfort in the notion that the company suffers from a case of institutional blindness, and blame the HR department or the CEO for all kinds of ills.

If you look closer, though, you begin to see how obvious it is that the self-defeaters' accusation of corporate blindness is really a red herring, even if they don't realize it themselves.

The *why* behind self-defeating behavior is not so obvious. Many of the chapters that follow describe how these behaviors have their roots in childhood. In fact, your personality is the repository of habits—both good and bad—that you learned in childhood.

In my "Get Out of Your Own Way" seminars and workshops, I use two charts to explain how and why self-defeating behavior develops (see appendices 1 and 2). The analysis of these charts goes as follows:

Success: Two Steps Forward, One Step Back

From your first breath to your last, you are stepping into the unknown. When you take that first baby step, it is daunting yet exhilarating. The real challenge to your evolving personality occurs when you take that first step and fall down. To be successful throughout your life, you want to make sure you take two steps forward and one step back, instead of one step forward (or no steps forward) and two steps back.

Think of an infant taking his first step. He crawls, then stands holding on to a chair or his parent's leg, and then ventures out into the world of *Homo erectus*. He steps away from any supports, balances precariously, looks back at his parent (developmental psychologists refer to this stage with the word *rapprochement*, which literally means "bringing together" or "reconciliation"). He feels reassured and ventures forth.

Sooner or later he falls and cries; one minute he felt like Superbaby, the next he found himself a helpless little creature. As powerful as he felt himself to be one moment was as fragile as he turned out to be in the next. He looked back at his parent for reassurance that what he had just experienced was a slip; it doesn't mean he has fallen through the cracks and it doesn't mean he can't get up and try again. Taking in his parent's reassurance, he *does* get up and try again. This occurs over and over until one day he is able to walk on his own.

When a child internalizes this new skill, a little piece of self-confidence develops and he integrates it into his evolving personality. As his personality develops into his own distinct identity, he becomes more and more an individual, and a confident one at that.

> One doesn't discover new lands without consenting
> to lose sight of shore for a very long time.
>
> —André Gide

THIS PROCESS CONTINUES all the way through life. One's personality and identity are constantly evolving in this two-steps-forward, one-step-back dance of learning—that is, falling, pausing, refueling, retooling, and retrying. Along the way, we make mistakes and learn from them; over time, we can develop perseverance, persistence, and effectiveness.

When you make forward progress, you feel vital, effective, and empowered, and you seek out opportunities to test your mettle in the world. The world is one giant opportunity and your oyster to explore and enjoy.

Self-Defeat: What Goes In, Comes Out

Now, let's talk about what happens to you when you defeat yourself. If as a baby you take that first step into the unknown, go to take a second step, fall, look back, and your parents do not respond to you with encouragement, you become stalled or, worse, slide further back (regress). You cannot proceed. You feel tentative, ineffective, disempowered. You seek out any mitigating behaviors that give you relief from these feelings. You adopt so-called "quick fixes," ways to cope that give you momentary relief from the trauma of falling from Superbaby to Powerless Baby, only to fix nothing and hurt you in the long run.

What happens when Superbaby is criticized (and feels as if he's done something wrong), ignored (and feels alone in his helplessness), or coddled (and then feels confused when not coddled)? Superbaby's reaction is fear, guilt, shame, anger, and confusion. He is suddenly and permanently knocked off the resilience track. He doesn't have the self-confidence he needs to get up and try again on his own. And instead of becoming effective, he seeks relief. Anything and everything he does in reaction to feeling "upset" triggers a negative coping reaction that works to make him feel better in the short run, but in the long run turns into a self-defeating behavior (SDB).

What's done to children, they will do to society.

—Karl Menninger

THESE BEHAVIORS waste time and squander his potential. Instead of seeing the world as a terrific place to explore, he views it as a terrifying place that can trip him up at every step. This causes him to stall in his life and his career. If he repeats these behaviors often enough, they become habits and eventually internalized parts of his personality that are very resistant to change. That is why you must not become discouraged if you are not able to stop and overcome these self-defeating behaviors overnight. Becoming impatient with yourself is in itself self-defeating.

The trick is to cut the endless playback loop of the old negative messages so that you can develop the inner strength and resolve to become effective in your life and work. This means replacing the abusive, critical, avoidant, neglectful, or overindulgent and enabling authoritarian voice in your head with the voice of the supportive, authoritative coach for yourself that you've always needed.

Human nature doesn't exist, only animal nature and the human potential to not give in to it.

—Source unknown

How to Use This Book

My consulting work has taken me to three levels of the corporate world: front-line salespeople, middle managers, and top executives.

Each group has different interests with regard to the origins of its self-defeating behavior.

In fact, one of the most counterproductive self-defeating behaviors I engaged in as I began working with businesspeople was my failure to take into consideration where my readers were coming from, which is why it's important for me to express how you might use this book.

If you focus on the bottom line at work—say, if you're a front-line salesperson—you may not be as interested in how or why my approach works as you are in simply using it to achieve better results. You may be solely interested in identifying your self-defeating behaviors, having realized the benefits of stopping and the cost of not stopping them. You may just want to cut to the chase. For you, the chapter titles and the action steps may be all you want or need.

If you are a middle manager, chances are you are a bottom-liner, too, but you also appreciate discovering strategies to mobilize and manage your people more effectively. You will be interested in how the approach in this book works, if not necessarily why it works. You will doubtless respond to the usable insights in the chapters that follow, thinking of them as other managers have as "pithy" add-ons to the action steps. The stories will also help to reinforce your learning because you may recognize in them yourself or the people who work for you.

If you are a senior executive, my hunch is that you will want to go deeper and discover why you, your family, and the people who work with you and for you engage in self-defeating behaviors. As a top manager, your understanding is a necessary component of leadership, because you function best when you know not only what works, but also how and why it works.

If, as a manager, the advice in this book seems especially relevant to your people, it will serve as a helpful vehicle for speaking with them about the self-defeating behaviors that are getting in their way. A particularly creative and effective approach I've seen has been when manager and subordinate use the "buddy system" and hold each other accountable for stopping an SDB. For instance, the manager may focus on stopping "Being Too Blunt" whereas the subordinate might select "Getting Defensive."

If you or someone who works for you views challenges on the job as "stressors" and copes with them by reverting to a self-defeating behavior, you are both limiting your chances for success. You give your peers and competitors carte blanche to pass you by. If, on the other hand, you use this book to support yourself and your employee, and to help yourselves more effectively confront and surmount the challenges that arise, you *will* both get out of your own way and be on your way to success neither of you ever dreamed of, or even believed possible. (For more specific advice regarding using this book, see appendix 3, "Twelve Steps to Getting Out of Your Own Way at Work.")

Finally, a note on the order of the chapters: Some self-destructive behaviors are more prevalent than others—at least, according to what I have witnessed among patients in my practice. I've ordered the chapters accordingly.

Here's to your future!

Chapter 1

Procrastinating

Procrastination is, hands down,
our favorite form of self-sabotage.

—Alyce P. Cornyn-Selby

WHEN I ASK ATTENDEES at training sessions to
identify what they need to do to become more successful
at their jobs, they name many things: "Get more sales," "Go
to more networking events," "Do more cold calls," "Spend
more time with clients," "Get to work earlier and leave
later." Rarely do they say, explicitly, "Stop procrastinating."

When I then ask them what would happen if they
stopped procrastinating on important tasks, they say, "It
would push my success to levels I can't imagine."

At work, procrastination is an epidemic, and one of the

most common self-sabotaging behaviors. It's one thing to procrastinate about something that affects you alone, such as going on a diet. It's another thing entirely to hinder the productivity of other people. When that happens, you're courting trouble and inviting resentment from others.

People have all kinds of reasons for procrastinating on the job. Some resent enslavement to a schedule. Other people feel overwhelmed by the task at hand or the amount of work they have to do. Still others procrastinate because their priorities aren't clear, or they're not sure how to begin—and they're afraid or ashamed to ask for help.

George, an editor at a national magazine, was a strong, erudite writer with total control of his particular subject matter, which happened to be the world of technology. But George would turn in his articles at the last minute. He would wait to develop an article until just a week or two before the production deadline—even in the case of articles that demanded serious research and reporting. He would sometimes pull all-nighters to get the piece in—and more than once put the production department in a tight squeeze.

When the magazine missed a shipping deadline and ran up a $10,000 bill in late fees to the printer, the production staff blamed George. He received a stern reprimand from the managing editor. "I don't care how talented you are," she told him. "Your procrastination is hurting other people and costing this company too much. Fix it, or else."

> Procrastination is one of the most common and deadliest
> of diseases and its toll on success and happiness is heavy.
> —Wayne Gretzky

AT ITS CORE, procrastination is not merely putting off *doing* something; it is putting off *making a decision*. It results from feeling overwhelmed. If you procrastinate, you have probably done things in the past that turned out badly or you received a negative reaction from authority figures—parents, teachers, coaches, or other adults. Over time, your fear of doing the wrong thing worsens. Fear of being punished overtakes your desire to take action. When you feel overwhelmed, you become paralyzed.

Procrastination can eventually push you up against a wall: The project you've been putting off must get done, or else. When the thought of being reprimanded or fired dawns on you at the last minute, an interesting thing occurs physiologically. You generate a massive out-pouring of adrenaline. Adrenaline is the body's natural attention-grabber. Adrenaline enables you to deal with a fight-or-flight situation. Your neurons suddenly line up and function flawlessly. You execute. (This may explain why so many people with attention deficit disorder are incredible procrastinators. When they do things at the last minute, they are self-medicating with the natural Ritalin of adrenaline.)

If you are like most people who procrastinate, you probably manage a last-minute save and "get away" with it. However, the problem worsens as you age, because the constant propulsion from the slow lane of procrastination to the fast lane of adrenaline-pumping takes a toll on your system. It messes with your stress hormones. You begin to lose your ability to pull off those last-minute saves.

George understood all of the above after I explained it to him, but still he didn't know what to do. We began talking about his son, Jake. Like many hard-driving, ambitious men, he had a real soft spot for his children, especially Jake. His son had true ADD. Like George, Jake did things at the last minute and was underachieving by leaps and bounds. His son was frustrated, angry, and discouraged about not being able to use his intelligence effectively. He once said to his dad, "What good is being smart when you can't use it? I wish I was stupid so I wouldn't have all that potential to live up to." George recognized in his son's pro-crastination some of the torment he himself felt.

I proposed that George take some of his busywork home and do it at the table alongside his son when Jake was doing his homework. "You could keep each other company doing things you both hate to do but know you need to do," I suggested.

George replied, "In a heartbeat. I'd do anything to help my kid feel better."

George and Jake began doing just that. They formally set aside time to work side by side on projects on which each had been procrastinating. Within a few months, the performance of both had improved. By working together, the tasks became tolerable.

> Teams share the burden and divide the grief.
>
> —Doug Smith

USABLE INSIGHT

We procrastinate not because we're lazy, but because we're overwhelmed.

⫸ Action Steps

1. *Ask a buddy for help.* When you feel overwhelmed, your ability to take action comes to a halt. Eliciting the assistance of a friend or coworker who's on your side but who doesn't "enable" you can help. Ask that friend to listen as you talk through your fears. Set up a regular time each week to check in with each other and hold each other accountable. (This is the principle behind twelve-step support groups.)

2. *Take it easy*—one task at a time. Select the top two tasks on which you are currently procrastinating that are important to your company. (Don't select more than two because lists of tasks are an invitation to procrastination.)

3. Continue to work with your buddy until the tasks on your priority list are done; then add two more activities and work together on those.

4. With practice, you will internalize the ability to talk yourself through the fear and come to rely more on yourself than on your buddy.

Chapter 2

Getting Defensive

I will permit no man to narrow and degrade
my soul by making me hate him.
>   —Booker T. Washington

QUICK QUIZ: When you get into an argument with
someone, do you (a) feel like the person on the other side
of the table is saying, "I'm right and you're wrong" (that is,
judging you unfairly), or (b) feel it's more important to say,
"I'm right and you're wrong" to the other person?

If you answered (a) you probably spend a lot of time
feeling defensive. When what you "hear" from someone
else is "I'm right and you're wrong"—whether or not that's
what they are really saying—you are taking offense. What
you may really want to say in response is, "God damn it! I

am not (always) wrong!" If you answered (b), you're spending too much of your time being self-righteous. You feel you are not *on* the attack but rather are feeling *under* attack.

Ironically, the person with whom you are arguing probably feels exactly the same thing you do. Neither of you wants to cause trouble (unless, of course, one or both of you are committed to being jerks). But both of you feel defensive because you have both felt offended. You and your combatant are exercising your rights to protect yourselves.

Recently, I was called in to intervene in a dispute between two high-level executives. I asked participants to ask each other, "Weren't you telling me I was wrong and you were right?" Both of them answered no. It was eye opening and poignant for each of them to discover that they were both defending themselves rather than attacking each other.

> If we could read the secret history of our enemies, we
> should find in each man's life sorrow and suffering
> enough to disarm any hostility.
> —Henry Wadsworth Longfellow

WHERE DOES all this trigger-happy defensiveness come from? Yet again, it's based on behaviors you learned as a child. If you felt your parents had a habit of telling you directly or indirectly that you were wrong—or worse, stupid, useless, and a loser—you carry into adulthood the belief that people are still saying those things to you (see "Why We Get in Our Own Way" in the introduction).

As a child, you were powerless to do much about this and may have cried or shut down or taken out your aggressions in the schoolyard. As an adult, however, you react differently. Something inside you rises up and, like the character played by Peter Finch in the movie *Network,* causes you to yell, "I'm mad as hell, and I'm not going to take it anymore!"

Your explosion is the cumulative result of holding back your hurt and subsequent anger from your childhood. And you're taking it out on someone in your present.

> Parents sometimes feel that if they don't criticize their child, their child will never learn. Criticism doesn't make people want to change; it makes them defensive.
>
> —Laurence Steinberg

HOW CAN YOU get over being defensive? In psychotherapy, patients sometimes experience what we in the profession call "transference." Patients react to a neutral therapist as if he or she were a person from the patient's past—typically a parent—who abused, neglected, or somehow mistreated them.

The work of therapy requires you first to recognize how you are transferring unresolved feelings toward people in your past onto your therapist (and no doubt onto others, especially authority figures) in the present. Over time, you develop enough presence of mind and self-awareness to recognize what you are doing and then purposefully stop doing it before it starts again.

Once you stop allowing your present relationships to pay for the sins of your past ones, you realize that being defensive—which springs from taking offense—only hurts your chances for success. By allowing your present relationships to be based on present reality, rather than to be haunted by dark past shadows, you'll find yourself much happier, not to mention much more successful as well.

⟫⟫⟫ Action Steps

1. Make a list of all the people at your job with whom you tend to argue.

2. Write the letter A next to a person's name if you believe he or she is saying to you, "I'm right and you're wrong."

3. Write the letter B if you believe the person is really saying, "I'm not wrong."

4. Approach the people you labeled B and ask them, "When we disagree, do you feel I am saying that I'm right and you're wrong, or are you really saying, 'I'm not wrong'?" Make it clear that you are not attacking them, but rather you are actually trying to clarify things.

5. Listen carefully to the person's response. You may be surprised to discover that what sounds like an attack isn't. This will encourage you.

6. Now, try the same thing with the people you labeled A. In the majority of cases, you will discover that even these people weren't attacking you, but rather being self-protective.

7. If you discover that people are telling you they are right and you are wrong, ask them to describe what specific behaviors they would suggest you change in order to correct what they say you are doing wrong. Whatever they say, don't become defensive. Just respond with a sincere "thank you." When they discover they have no one with whom to fight, the power will shift toward you.

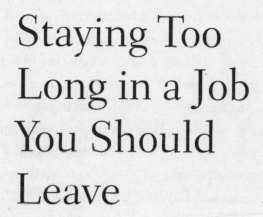

Chapter 3

Staying Too Long in a Job You Should Leave

> If you have made a mistake, cut your losses
> as quickly as possible.
>
> —Bernard Baruch

YOU'RE NOT A SLACKER. You get your work done. But you identify completely with Dilbert. You go to bed on Sunday, dreading the Monday morning alarm. You check the clock in the afternoon, anticipating leaving at your earliest opportunity. When you're at work, you take every opportunity to walk the halls, chat with colleagues. You leave early if you can or play around on the Internet until others start to leave. You call in sick when you're not.

"So you think your job is awful? Well, listen to this!" opens the subject of many an inebriated evening, as well as the theme of many a Hollywood script.

It's amazing how many highfliers have done time in stinky jobs. I know one fellow, now a Ph.D. in economics, whose job was to crush frozen turkey skulls in a giant vat to make cat food. Or the professor at an Ivy League university who worked the graveyard shift serving midnight coffee to drunks who threw up in the cream holder and then fell asleep in the booth. The federal judge who worked from ten P.M. to six A.M. cutting up film negatives (at least she got free entertainment in the bargain). And then there was the famous director who worked as a garbage man and once fainted from the stink. Admittedly, they held all these jobs in high school and college, but they suffered all the same.

So now you're in a stinky job. You're not exactly goofing off, but meaning, learning, and fun have long since fled. You need to keep working to pay the bills. You wish you could find a way out, but you're so trapped by your need for your paycheck that you haven't got the time and energy to think your way out of the box.

> I shall tell you a great secret, my friend. Do not wait for
> the Last Judgment. It takes place every day.
>
> —Albert Camus

So why don't you cut your losses? There are many possible reasons:

➤ *Not having a plan.* You've put all your eggs in one basket and can't see an alternative. You're in survival mode: You feel so tired and trapped that the mere thought of gathering the energy to look for another job is itself debilitating. (This is the same psychological effect that keeps people in bad marriages. The devil they know is bad, but the devil they don't know is simply too daunting to consider.)

➤ *Not wanting to feel like you're a quitter.* You may just be a glutton for punishment. But if you're not, you are glued to your employer by a feeling of guilt, and ironically because it's in your employer's interest to keep you feeling guilty.

➤ *Being optimistic.* Hope springs eternal. Maybe you want to believe that the positive change you think, want, and will to happen, will happen—even if it's painfully obvious that nothing will change. You can't accept that you are not going to get anything meaningful for the time and effort you have already put into your work.

➤ *Not wanting to be wrong.* If you went for the so-called "dream job" that has turned out to be disappointing or worse, you may have doubts about your judgment in other areas. If you fail at this, you may ask yourself, what *can* I succeed at?

➤ *Thinking that you can't do anything else.* If you feel that you have the job you deserve and you don't deserve any better, you remain where you are.

How do you break out of your box? What's the difference between the people who have moved on to better things and those who haven't?

> Unless you move, the place where you are is the place you will always be.
>
> —Ashleigh Brilliant

THE MOST critical difference between success and failure is envisioning that your life *can* be different and taking the actual steps, however small, to move toward that dream. Even the tiniest thing that inspires you and makes you feel happy—volunteering at church, working with animals, taking a night class—makes a huge difference in moving your attitude toward a more positive place. It breaks through to your motivation; since you are putting your body on the road to where you want to go, it can pull the rest of you along.

Bruce Wright, founder of the consulting firm Macro Strategic Design, helps people to achieve the best life possible so that at the end they have no regrets. Here's one of the exercises he proposes:

Close your eyes and imagine you have $50 million. It's all legal, tax free, and yours to do with as you choose. With that sum, you would never have to do anything that you don't want to do again. So, what would you do?

Some people say they would travel extensively; others say they would buy several homes. Others would focus on making the world better. What would you do?

When you open your eyes, think of small things you can already do down the path you envisioned *without having that wealth*. This means that you can plan more trips, lease (or time-share) a residence in another city for part of the year, or give time to one of the worthy charities in your area. In other words, you can start living the way you want to, now.

Once your mind opens up and your attitude shifts, formulate a plan. The artists, academics, and other achievers I mentioned above all had plans. None of these people saw their situation as the end, merely as a means. Of course, when you are middle-aged, the distinction becomes muddier because you have more responsibilities. But I have yet to see a determined person of reasonable intelligence and equipped with a plan fail to move on to better things.

>>> Action Steps

1. To tell if a situation is one in which you should cut your losses, ask yourself, "If I had it to do all over again, would I? If so, why? If not, why not? And why am I continuing to keep trying?"

2. Before you put more time and effort into any situation, ask yourself, "What's the evidence that things will turn out any differently now?" And "What can I do to avoid making it a total loss?"

3. Ask yourself, "What's the worst thing that will happen if I just cut my losses now? Is it any worse than if I don't and things continue to deteriorate?" And "If I did stop doing this, what energy, time, and money would it free up for me to do something else?"

4. Don't complain unless you are taking action. Complaining only keeps you wedded to where you are and alienates you from the people who want to support you because you're boring. The goal is to get others to root for you—and then root harder when you get closer to career fulfillment.

5. To get out of survival mode, find a way to do something—anything—that you truly enjoy and that might pave the way to another career or job. Consider doing something you would love to do but never thought you could because you didn't have the background, and then volunteer to learn more about it. (If you feel too trapped to take the time off, think again: The time you invest in enjoying something new will be repaid in time subtracted from your current stress.)

6. Get support. Remember that the more support you get, the more progress you will make.
7. Set a time limit. If things don't get better in a month, start polishing your résumé and doing some serious job searching, and enroll in a night class.

Chapter 4

Taking the Bait

But for every man there exists a bait which
he cannot resist swallowing.

—Friedrich Nietzsche

I ONCE CONDUCTED a training workshop for forty
top financial managers at a large company that handled
more than $60 billion in client assets. The challenge I set
them was this: Persuade a high-net-worth person to leave
a competitor and instead sign on with their company. "I've
got twenty-five million dollars in assets under management at your competitor," I told the assembled group. "It
used to be thirty-five million before your competitor helped
me blow it in the dot-com bubble. Now I'm thinking of
switching to your side."

Everyone in the room smiled a self-satisfied smile, nodding as if I'd just made a very intelligent decision.

"But," I continued, "why should I change to your company when it's nearly identical to my present financial management firm? After all, your mission statement is almost the same as theirs—it's twenty percent sincere, eighty percent sales pitch."

The faces lost their smiles, but being the competitive types that they were, they prepared themselves to meet my challenge.

"I bet you don't even know what your mission statement is, much less practice it," I said accusingly.

The mouths tightened with hostile determination.

"In fact," I went on, "you've lost as much money for some of your clients as my current company has lost for me. So why should I give my money to you?"

Every adviser in the room responded to my gauntlet. They told me how they diversify their clients' investments and do a full assessment of their clients' risk tolerance. They extolled the name of their company and how it had been around for more than a hundred years. And yada yada yada.

The audience of financial managers clearly didn't know that they had been baited. I had deliberately provoked them into arguing with me. My goal was to demonstrate how quickly they went into defensive and argumentative mode. Instead of trying to sell me persuasively by (as Steven Covey would say) "seeking first to understand, and then be understood," they were reacting to my testiness.

Watching their reaction to me, the managing director who had arranged for me to speak could barely hide his amusement. In the debriefing and didactic portion of my training that followed this session, I pointed out how quickly they'd launched a counterattack. The seniormost managing director broke in. "Amazing!" he said to the audience. "This guy baited all of you and every one of you took it. How do you expect the level of client we deal with to respect you—much less sign over their assets—if you do that?"

> Better shun the bait, than struggle in the snare.
>
> —John Dryden

PEOPLE AT WORK are baited all the time. Baiting is a form of insult that takes various forms. Sometimes, it is merely teasing, a bit of banter that catches you naïvely off-guard. Sometimes, it's less innocent, as in the kind of sexual innuendo that most companies frown upon. Sometimes, it's deliberately provocative: I know of several technology companies in which the senior managers try to get their engineers to publicly defend their decisions. And sometimes, it's downright hostile, and the insults are real and barbed.

In all cases, it feels as if the people who are doing the baiting are the ones in control of the situation, and when you're on the receiving end, you feel you have to react to regain your own control. It may feel natural to get defensive. But if you do, and act before you think, you can lose twice. Getting into a defensive argument costs you respect in the eyes of the other person, and later on your self-respect as you feel dragged down to their level.

In 1996, I witnessed a wonderful example of someone who refused to take the bait.

"General Powell, I understand that your wife once suffered from depression, had to take medicine, and was even in a mental hospital. Do you want to comment on that?"

You could hear all eight thousand people in the Dallas Civic Auditorium sucking in their breath. They could hardly believe their ears. Everyone went quiet.

Colin Powell had just opened the question-and-answer period after delivering a stirring, inspiring keynote address at the national conference for a leading residential real estate company's top producers. At the time, Powell was being considered as a serious choice for the presidential nomination. He had urged the audience of hard-driving agents and brokers to give back to their communities. He had passionately spoken of his gratitude for his family and childhood friends. As he spoke of opportunities "to do well by doing good," he entreated the audience to do the same.

"Inappropriate" was too kind a word for the off-the-wall question hurled at Powell. We all wondered how the general would react. I remembered that Edmund Muskie had thrown away his presidential hopes twenty-five years earlier when someone in an audience asked about *his* wife's mental problems, and the Maine senator started to cry. Would Powell react emotionally? Would he ignore the man? Would he become hostile?

Instead, he simply responded: "Excuse me. The person you love more than anyone is living in hell, and *you* don't do whatever you can to get her out? Do you have a problem with that, sir?"

You could hear a pin drop. "Talk about leadership!" I said to myself. "I'd buy a used country from that guy!"

> Water is fluid, soft, and yielding. But water will wear
> away rock, which is rigid and cannot yield. As a rule,
> whatever is fluid, soft, and yielding will overcome
> whatever is rigid and hard. This is another paradox:
> what is soft is strong.
>
> —Lao-Tzu

POWELL DIDN'T take the bait because he spoke from the principle of doing the right thing rather than from ego and having to be right. If you practice identifying what the right thing to do is and have that dictate your actions, you, too, will find yourself centered whenever you are challenged or baited.

I had admired Powell before, but after witnessing his response I felt inspired to be the best I could be. He also embedded in my memory the fact that not taking the bait is one of the greatest ways to earn respect.

There are many situations in the workplace where people bait you. Whether or not you take it and blow a chance to gain respect is up to you.

USABLE INSIGHT

When you take the bait, you not only lose your cool—you lose the chance to earn respect.

>>> Action Steps

1. Identify the situations in your life in which you are most likely to be baited and the people most likely to do the baiting.
2. Rather than trying to win with them, instead adopt the principle of doing what is fair and reasonable as your guide.
3. When baited, instead of reacting, remain quiet (but pleasant) and say nothing.
4. The people baiting you will most likely become agitated and confront you again. Let them do so. Remain calmly on the high road.

5. Your response to baiting should go something like this: "It's clear to me that you're upset or frustrated with me, but less clear what it's about. Tell me what it is you'd like me to do going forward, and if it's fair and reasonable to me and you and everyone it affects, I'll be happy to oblige. If it's not fair and reasonable, I'm going to have a problem with it." In all likelihood, they'll back off or go bait someone else, in which case you're off the hook.

Chapter 5

Not
Delegating

Surround yourself with the best people
you can find. Delegate authority and
don't interfere.

—Ronald Reagan

"**WE'RE TAKING YOU OFF** the respirator," the chief
resident in Surgery told Fred, a man who had undergone
extensive head and neck surgery after a car accident. Fred
had lived with the hated breathing tube in his neck for a
whole month. He kept writing us notes asking how long
before it could be taken out. But now faced with the reality
that the tube was coming out, he was far from relieved.
Instead, he was terrified by the thought that he wouldn't
be able to breathe on his own.

The next day, Fred's eyes were wide as saucers as we calmly tried to reassure him that he would be able to breathe through his mouth. Slowly we removed the tube connected to the tracheotomy opening in his neck. Fred was so frightened he dug his nails into his attending doctor's forearms, drawing blood.

Finally, he took the first breath on his own. We all breathed easier after that.

Even though Fred knew he needed to get off the respirator if he was to continue to recover, he was scared to let go.

Overly dramatic as this scenario may seem, it's the way some people feel when it is time to delegate a task to someone else in order for them to take the next step in their career. Take the case of Julia, a very competent project specialist for a small architectural firm. Julia was a smart, can-do person who took a lot of pleasure and pride in her work. She enthusiastically took on new projects and volunteered to help other people with theirs. The overall effect was fine, at first. She received rave reviews from her bosses and a raise.

But as she dug into her work, she found her to-do list getting longer. Papers piled up in her in-box and her e-mails multiplied. She found herself working longer and longer hours. Even when her boss suggested she pass on a project or two to a colleague, she refused. Sometimes she'd forget requests altogether. This left her colleagues stuck with having to play catch-up on her to-do list. As they discovered more and more neglected or overlooked tasks, they began to resent her failure to keep up with her work. Finally her boss took her off several projects and reassigned them to others, to Julia's humiliation.

Of course, Julia is not alone. Delegation is unbelievably difficult for a lot of people, and for many different reasons. Some of these aren't of our own making. First of all, many work environments discourage delegation, either openly or subliminally. Most companies have tried to save money by cutting back on administrative staff. The result is that everyone but the most senior managers acts as their own gofers—running to the copy machine, refilling the printer paper, scheduling meetings, and so on—wasting a lot of time that they might spend more productively.

Companies also expect people to pull their own weight. While bosses are only too happy to assign more and more work, we internalize the thinking that asking for help is a sign of weakness. So we bravely slog on. We're pressured for time, so we think that we don't have the time to bring someone else up to speed.

But the failure to delegate can also be of our own making. The reasons have to do with psychological control issues. People who refuse to delegate often have problems with trust. Julia, for instance, was the child of an alcoholic who felt she had to hold her dysfunctional family together. Even as a child, she cooked and cleaned while her mother slept it off. Since she didn't win attention from her mother, she won it at school from her teachers. She was the classic "good kid" who won kudos for her industriousness and hard work. She identified so much with her work and with the tasks at hand that if anyone suggested she do less or allow someone else to take over, she felt devalued. At the same time, she truly believed the adage that "if you want something done right, you have to do it yourself." Not being able to trust her parent to act like an adult evolved, in her own adulthood, into not being able to trust other adults.

In the workplace this lack of trust can translate into a failure to live up to one's own expectations of one's self. Julia really believed that she was the most competent project coordinator in the place, and that she was management material. In setting out to prove it, she developed a sense that she was indispensable (see "Thinking You're Indispensable"). But what she really worried about was what would happen if she failed to handle everything on her plate. Ironically, she sabotaged herself by doing just that.

> The best executive is the one who has sense enough
> to pick good men to do what he wants done, and
> self-restraint enough to keep from meddling
> with them while they do it.
>
> —Theodore Roosevelt

BUT JULIA *did* learn to delegate. She did it by following the example of Fred at the beginning of this chapter. What enabled Fred to summon the trust to let go of the respirator (it didn't hurt the equation that he didn't have a choice) was that the doctors had presented him with a calm, logical, step-by-step plan to help him make the transition from not breathing on his own to breathing on his own. For every step of the way, Fred followed the plan that allowed him to pause and "catch his breath" until he had "delegated" his breathing from a machine to his lungs. Had there not been a "way" for him to do it, he would have had much more trouble summoning the "will" to do it.

One of the ways Julia learned to delegate was to follow the procedure we used in our medical training when it was time for a resident to delegate a task to an intern. It was called "See one, do one, teach one." In this exercise an intern would watch as the resident taught him a procedure. Next the intern would do the procedure under the resident's supervision, describing what he was doing each step of the way. Finally the intern would teach the procedure to the medical student and the process would continue. Ultimately, the intern taught the procedure enough that he "owned" it.

Once Julia learned to view the task to be delegated as a procedure for someone else to see, do, and teach, she was able to bridge the trust gap and finally delegate.

⟫⟫⟫ Action Steps

1. Think of the task you want to delegate.
2. Set aside time to have the person to whom you are delegating:
    *   see you do what they need to do;
    *   do it themselves under your supervision;
    *   "teach" you or someone else how to do it.
3. At first, it will still be difficult for you to follow these steps, but once you have followed them, it will have lessened your worries enough about what will happen to allow you to let go of the task.
4. If you're thinking that you can't break the task down into something you can teach because it is so intuitively ingrained in you, take a deep breath and try again or take a break and come back to it. You will see that you can do it.

Chapter 6

Talking Over or At Others

A gentleman, nurse, that loves to hear
himself talk, and will speak more in a minute
than he will stand to in a month.
      —William Shakespeare, *Romeo and Juliet*

IN SHAKESPEARE'S PLAY, Romeo's best friend, Mercutio, habitually works himself into a lather by talking, talking, talking. He gets so caught up in his own verbal flights of fancy that he completely forgets where he is or who is listening to him or what kind of trouble his words have gotten him into. Instead of "standing to" and defending the goal of reason between the bitterly feuding families, he's self-entranced. He can't stop talking even when he's bleeding to death.

Mercutio, at least, was clever and entertaining. Not everyone is so gifted. People who talk over or at others are not just boring—they're downright alienating. They don't give a damn about the receiving end. Worse, they completely ignore the signals that their would-be listeners are sending them.

I'll never forget a Mercutio-like fellow who liked to take over weekly meetings. David saw these encounters as competitive matches and as opportunities to one-up his colleagues. He would cut people off, interjecting what he thought was a clever observation, and then spend ten minutes tediously explaining his transparent logic. If he'd stopped at the mere observation, his colleagues might have been curious and asked him to go on. If he'd offered just a minute or two of thoughtful explanation, they might have respected him. But by assuming and then controlling the floor, he earned nothing but rolling eyes, exchanged glances, and checked watches. He didn't notice that he was irritating everyone until his boss suggested that he try holding back a little. He finally stopped talking so much, but it took some time to regain the respect of his colleagues. He was Mercutio without the talent.

Fundamentally, people who talk too much are insecure and screaming for attention. They didn't get noticed at home, and it shows through their lime-green egos. They turn into their parents, lecturing instead of listening. They also believe that if they talk on long enough, they will deflect attention from the fact that they really *are* insecure. But the reality is that they're not fooling anyone. David, for example, craved respect, but privately he didn't feel he deserved it because as a child he felt ignored and that no one respected him. By talking over and at others, he only focused a spotlight on his own problem.

> The time to stop talking is when the other person nods
> his head affirmatively but says nothing.
>
> —Vince Havner

IT WAS no surprise that David had no friends at work. No one asked him to lunch because no one enjoys a one-way conversation. One day, at the end of a meeting in which he had blathered on, he overheard two colleagues talking about him. "My God, can't he just shut *up*?" one of them said. "How stupid does he think we are?" David, of course, was shocked and upset. That's when he came to see me.

The first step in David's recovery was to start thinking about the way he communicated. I explained to him that all of us have a default mode when we communicate, particularly at work. These default modes are *monologue, diatribe, argument, discussion*, and *dialogue*.

David's default mode was *monologue*. It was as if he were onstage, like Mercutio. He talked as if listeners were a captive audience.

A *diatribe* is an angry monologue. In a diatribe, you're venting, or ranting, and you're under the impression that yours is the only view that matters (see "Confusing Dumping with Venting"). If you have any emotional intelligence, you leave the meeting feeling vaguely embarrassed but defensive of your ego. (Warning: Ego always trumps honesty, unless you sincerely want to change.)

In an *argument*, you and your listener are equals, but you see your listener as merely an enemy combatant. It's target practice. Your listener shoots at you, and you shoot back in a war of one-upmanship, no weakness or faltering allowed.

The more you know, the less you need to say.

—Jim Rohn

AT WORK, we all want to be engaged in a *discussion*. In this scenario, we're all in college. The communication is clear and calm, with equal weight being given to all sides. Discussion is an intellectual process, preferably with a professorial guide to help with Socratic questions. This is the kind of communication we aim for in meetings. Unfortunately, discussions can be hijacked by people who want to command the environment by launching into monologues, diatribes, or arguments. (There goes Socrates.)

I've observed that true leaders, or leaders to be, have learned the art of *dialogue,* which is person-to-person communication. Dialogue is the art of disregarding status. It's not just about the board member on the golf course who wants you to drive the shot his way, or the department head following orders. It goes beyond the mutual respect that causes you to talk *to* each other, and reaches into the genuine regard that leads you to talk *with* one another.

Dialogue starts with empathy, a capacity most of us have but too many of us do not use because we're so busy defending our egos. When you're engaged in a true dialogue, your ego isn't invested because you're more concerned with understanding than dominating the other person. Dialogue springs from empathy, which is the basis of teamwork: When you notice the stress in the guy on the manufacturing line and reach out to him, the team performs better. Dialogue is also the stuff of great marriages. You are connected emotionally as well as mentally to your spouse, and you're willing to listen and learn. As you move into dialogue, frustration and resentment give way to hope and graciousness. Both you and your spouse feel that you understand each other. You connect.

If you want to improve your standing among colleagues, you need to turn off the switches that want to go into monologue, diatribe, and argument, and turn on the discussion and dialogue switches.

》》》 Action Steps

1. *Check your style by the response you're getting.* It's not easy to stop the talking-over-or-at habit, but it can be done by using your powers of observation to help you. The key is to watch the way people listen to you. By paying close attention to their body language, you can tell what kind of communication style you're using. Next time you're in a meeting, watch the signals you're receiving and try to match them to your communication style.

2. *Check for the removal of the monologue.* When you are engaged in a monologue, the person on the receiving end will demonstrate *removed* listening, which really isn't listening at all. When you're at work and the person you are talking to is removed, you will notice that they look away, as if they are looking for an exit, or nod absently.

3. *Check for the defensiveness of the diatribe.* When you are engaged in a diatribe, you will see two different kinds of facial responses, depending on the personality of the person you are talking over. People who resent diatribes will shift the planes of their faces upward at you and tighten their lips or stick out their chins ("Boy, are you full of yourself," they're thinking). Those who feel abused or intimidated by your diatribe will shift the plane of their faces downward, tucking in their chin in a submissive reflex, as if to say, "I'm stuck. I'll just wait until this is over."

4. *Check for the reaction of argument.* When you are engaged in

an argument, the person listening to you is defiant. Their form of listening is *reactive,* which occurs when people use each other as verbal punching bags, bouncing off what the other says in a defensive, combative, or condescending manner. The body language you see will appear resentful. (If you have a teenager who reacts angrily just about every time you open your mouth, you get the idea.)

5. *Aim for the responsiveness of discussion.* During a respectful discussion, the person listening to you is attentive and respectful, and their listening is *responsive.* Responsive listeners respectfully hear you out and are actively trying to understand the content of what you're saying. The discussion mode is also interactive, as in a meeting when everyone is contributing points of view. When you are in discussion mode, you will notice that your listeners have their necks up and are looking directly at you without shifting their gaze. You may detect a knitted brow or a narrowed gaze. They may not agree with what you are saying, but their body language is not confrontational.

6. *Aim for the connection of dialogue.* In a true dialogue, your respondent is in a connective mode. When someone feels they're equally engaged with you, both emotionally and intellectually, there is a sense of mutual curiosity, respect, and regard. Your listener looks animated. Because they trust you, they are visibly relaxed.

Remember, less is more. Think of the wisest person you ever met—a favorite relative, a minister or rabbi, a great teacher—and try to recall *how* they listened to you. What did their faces do as you spoke? How responsive were they to your questions? Did they interrupt you, or did they hear you out? Chances are that the wise person was an excellent listener; they may have understood that it's more important to speak well than to speak at all.

Chapter 7

Being Competent but Out of Touch

> You cannot depend on your eyes when your
> imagination is out of focus.
>
> —Mark Twain

IN MY PRACTICE I see many people who are technically competent at their jobs. By this I mean that they have all the skills necessary to do their jobs, such as crunching numbers or programming software. They're good at what they do.

But as competent as they are, such people often lack charm. They're not good with people. In fact, they aren't really interested in other people. If anything, they complain about the fact that other people succeed who are less capable than they are.

People who are competent in this way—that is, who assume they have all the answers on a technical or procedural level—often lack emotional intelligence (EI), or the awareness of usually unspoken wants, needs, and fears in others and in oneself. This inability to understand emotional signals significantly influences business interactions. Without EI, it's as if you are listening on just one channel.

> Competence, like truth, beauty, and contact lenses,
> is in the eye of the beholder.
>
> —Dr. Laurence J. Peter

I'VE NOTICED that the higher people go in organizations, the more inured they often become to input from other people (see "Being Closed Off to Input"). As children, folks like this typically excelled in school. Pushed hard, often by micromanaging but emotionally unavailable parents, these "good" students suffer from stunted emotional intelligence. Kids who are smart but emotionally ignored learn that they can earn praise from parents, teachers, and other adults by collecting good grades, certificates, awards, trophies, medals, and other outward signs of success. But if they aren't equally encouraged to connect with other people on a gut level, they can grow insensitive.

Once they get to where they're going, their emotional deafness worsens. As overachievers, they begin to feel they are the only people with opinions worth listening to. It's difficult for them to respect others. Focused on proving their own competence, they ignore subtle yet important signals. Resentment against them builds, and sometimes self-sabotage can follow.

> We don't see things as they are, we see them as we are.
>
> —Anaïs Nin

TAKE THE EXAMPLE of Leonard, a senior manager who had been hired by a thriving, family-owned supply business. Leonard was a brilliant project manager who had outsold virtually every other salesperson at a huge national firm. He was, by all accounts, a sales rock star, and the founder/CEO was overjoyed to have him on the team.

Competent as he was, Leonard had a dark side. Fiercely competitive, he avoided opportunities to socialize with colleagues. He was miserly in his praise of others' work. "Good" was the best he could ever muster for a colleague's plan. But as a critic, he was enthusiastically caustic. On one memo, he wrote: "Do not do this to me again." On another, he scribbled: "Hiring mistake?" Occasionally, a staffer would complain of Leonard's treatment to his boss. But Leonard didn't appear to care. Focused exclusively on bringing in sales and climbing to the rank of executive vice president, he blithely ignored them all.

During the annual review process, Leonard was convinced that they would be eager to promote him. But his review got delayed. The boss procrastinated, since he was reluctant to confront Leonard about his poor interpersonal skills and didn't want to risk provoking him. Eventually Leonard and his boss did meet, and Leonard learned that the HR department had recommended against a promotion.

True to his boss's prediction, this news infuriated Leonard. He dashed off a letter to his former boss at his previous company, explaining that he was considering quitting. Unfortunately, he left a copy of the letter in the printer. You can guess how this story ended.

Why do competent people like Leonard—and possibly like you—self-sabotage themselves in this way? Oftentimes it is because their self-worth is directly tied to their sense of competence.

I've observed that people who are highly competent in technical areas are frequently much less competent in interpersonal matters. They resist being pulled out of their comfort zone, and their resistance usually manifests itself as hostility. Often these people turn out to be secretly shy; they overcompensate for their shyness with a show of competence. (Interestingly, they often jump to agree with my analysis of their shyness and seem relieved to have it identified.)

Your secret shyness may cause you to feel not just uncomfortable, but also incompetent and defenseless. You may avoid situations that cause you to feel shy. As a result, you have a difficult time not only in giving sincere thank-yous, apologies, and congratulations, but also in receiving them.

What can you do? You can wait until your incompetence with people overtakes your know-it-all-ness and bushwhacks your career, as happened to Leonard. But you don't have to. Instead, you can learn how to tune in to others.

If you suffer from more than five of the misconceptions about others or yourself in either of the charts below, you're hurting your success. The following will assist you in being mindful of the many misconceptions that can complicate your interpersonal relationships.

10 Misconceptions
of How Others View You

What You Think You Are	What They Really Think You Are
Shrewd	Sly
Confident	Arrogant
Humorous	Inappropriate

Energetic	Hyper
Having strong opinions	Opinionated
Passionate	Impulsive
Strong	Rigid
Detail-oriented	Nitpicky
Quiet	Passive
Flexible	Indecisive

10 Misconceptions You May Have About Others

When You Think They Are	They May Really Be
Moved by passion	Moved by facts
Moved by facts	Moved by passion
Fun-loving	Serious
Serious	Fun-loving
Looking for a reason to buy in	Looking for a reason to buy out
Looking for a reason to buy out	Looking for a reason to buy in
Wanting to be told	Wanting to be asked
Needing to be convinced	Ready to buy
Ready to buy	Needing to be convinced
Excited about your company (work?)	Thinking your company is (you are?) a dog

>>> Action Steps

1. Review the two charts above and count the number of misconceptions you have about others, or they have about you.

2. Select people who have misconceptions.

3. Approach each of them and say something like, "I realize that I may be misperceiving some things. For instance, I may kid you about things that I think are funny that actually may rub you the wrong way or even offend you. Is that true? What effect does that have on your feelings about working for me?"

4. After you hear their response, do not become defensive. Instead respond with: "Really? I didn't know it was having such a bad effect. I'm going to try to stop it."

5. Remember, people will root more for you if you are a reformed jerk than if you are a nice guy because it feels so great to stop being afraid of or angry at you. When that happens, they will put out much more effort for you—and help you to succeed.

Chapter 8

Not
Listening

It is the province of knowledge to speak, and
it is the privilege of wisdom to listen.

—Oliver Wendell Holmes

I **ATTENDED** an executive-level conference in which
the people in the room were asked to turn to their neighbor and say one thing they wished they could do better.
My neighbor turned to me and said, with a twinge of
embarrassment and guilt in his eyes, "I wish I was a better
listener."

I could practically hear the voices in his head—probably those of his wife and kids—telling him he didn't listen.

Listening is one of the most important things we can
possibly do because it is the one skill people most want

from us. Sadly, few of us are very good at it. No wonder—our world is so full of noise that it seems we have to shout to hear ourselves above the din. And when so many demands are made on us, listening feels like a luxury.

It's fairly easy to separate good listeners from bad ones. If you watch people, you can easily divide their listening skills into the four R's: removed, reactive, responsible, and receptive.

Removed listening is the saddest kind of non-listening. It's the sad non-interaction you often see between an old married couple who probably should have separated long ago and now barely tolerate each other: One spouse natters on while the other reads the paper or watches television. The person who isn't listening is absorbed in something else. People who are removed listeners feel overrun (or anticipate feeling that way) and preemptively distance themselves. Their removal is self-preserving: They feel that if they start listening they will drown in the noise coming at them and react by getting angry. So they just shut down.

In business settings, removed listeners are the people who sit around in meetings checking their watches. They don't want to cooperate; they have better things to do. (If you talk *over* or *at* people, you'll get removed listening in return.)

> You cannot truly listen to anyone and do anything else
> at the same time.
>
> —M. Scott Peck

REACTIVE LISTENING is a highly subjective, emotionally charged form of non-listening. People who are reactive listeners tend to take things personally and respond in a variety of ways. They may be overly sensitive, hearing what is said as a criticism or indictment (see "Being Thin-Skinned"). Or they may respond impulsively, speaking before they think (see "Being Impulsive"). If you are a reactive listener at work, you're a live wire; others may feel that you are too difficult to deal with.

Responsible listening is what most of us *should* engage in at work: It's a no-nonsense, purposeful exchange of information. Responsible listeners listen for the facts in order to move forward. If your CEO gives you instructions and you listen responsibly, you say, "Yup, got it," and can work with the information to get something done well and appropriately. Your CEO will appreciate your concise response and, if you follow through, you may be seen as promotion material.

> It takes two to speak the truth: one to speak
> and another to hear.
>
> —Henry David Thoreau

RECEPTIVE LISTENING is listening of the highest order, and it is the human listening that all of us crave. It's empathic: Receptive listeners are able to "hear between the words." Receptive listeners see and then feel where you're coming from. Wilfred Bion, one of the preeminent psychoanalysts of the twentieth century, described this as "listening without memory or desire." He explained that when you listen to someone with memory you're trying to fit them into an old agenda of yours; when you listen with desire, you're trying to fit them into a new agenda. When you listen without either you are completely open to what they are communicating verbally and nonverbally.

To understand these levels better, imagine a child coming to your door, soaked, chilled, and convulsively shivering. The *removed* listener doesn't even answer the doorbell. The *reactive* listener blames and then lectures the child for being out in the rain. The *responsible* listener says, "Oh, you're wet" and then asks obvious questions: "Are you cold? Would you like to dry off and warm up?"

The *receptive* listener, on the other hand, sees and knows what's happened. He invites the child in and says, "Jeez, you must be freezing. Come in. Here's a warm blanket and some dry clothes for you to change into." In this last case, the child is taken inside spontaneously without having to go through a litany of questions, explain the obvious, or go into a long description of what happened. Her needs have been anticipated and met.

It's not impossible to train yourself to be a receptive listener, but first you need to overcome some bad habits that may have developed over a lifetime, usually as a reaction to feeling like you haven't been listened to yourself. This first requires you to become an active listener—that is, you must observe how you listen to others, and observe others as they listen to you. By keeping tabs on how you feel when others are speaking to you, and sorting their listening styles into buckets, you can aim higher.

Do some bucket-sorting on yourself, too: If people look anywhere but at you when you are speaking, they're removing themselves (and before you react against this, ask yourself how you might be speaking that causes them to do so). If they look at you directly in an engaged way, you're getting through in a way that makes them receptive.

USABLE INSIGHT

The more you listen to where people are coming from, the more they'll let you take them where you want them to go.

>>> Action Steps

1. Look into people's eyes when they're speaking to you.
2. As a person is speaking, fill in these blanks in your mind:
   a. What he/she is saying to me is _____.
   b. The reason he/she is telling me is _____.
   c. What he/she is hoping I will do after I hear him/her is _____.
   d. What he/she worries I might do after I hear the statement is _____.
   e. Ask the person whether the answers are correct. Each time you are correct, the person will say "yes" and feel understood. Consequently the person will become more open to you.
   f. If your answers are incorrect, ask the person to clarify, then repeat the clarification, beginning with: "So, what you're saying to me is really _____."

Chapter 9

Lacking Self-Discipline

> First we make our habits, then our habits
> make us.
>
> —Charles C. Noble

PHIL, a graphic designer, was a really creative fellow. Unfortunately, he always seemed to be skating on the edge of failure. He tended to be late for work. When at work, he'd flit from one project to another without really zeroing in on one. He was personally unkempt, as was his work space. This furthered the impression that he wasn't in control—or that he didn't care.

His supervisor was fairly tolerant, being a creative type herself, and she thought Phil was the most talented person on her team. But he always seemed to be more frenzied and overwhelmed than he needed to be. There was always some minor flaw in his designs that could easily have been prevented if he'd checked his work completely before presenting it.

Though the errors ultimately didn't hurt the product, his teammates resented the fact that they had to clean up after him. They viewed his sloppiness as more than carelessness; they felt he was arrogant in assuming everything would be fixed and excused.

Phil was productive enough to not be in danger of losing his job, but he was never in danger of being promoted, either. Each time he received a performance review, his boss would remind him that he needed to be more disciplined. If he'd plan out his projects better, she told him, he wouldn't be so hurried. She enrolled him in a time management course, which seemed to improve matters, but only for a short time. It wasn't long before Phil slipped into his old bad habits.

Phil himself talked about his need to be more conscientious. If he was late to a meeting or made a mistake, he'd apologize and say, "I wish I were more self-disciplined! I really have to work on that." This became his mantra.

One day Phil received a less than understanding response from his boss. "Phil, stop complaining about your lack of self-discipline," she said tersely. "I feel like you're trying to manipulate me into letting you off the hook every time you say it. I'm not going to support you until you do something about it. Either change your behavior or just shut up."

Phil was taken aback. He was about to shoot something back defensively, but he was so—as the young interns at the company would say—"busted," there was nothing he could say. Some people have a legitimate excuse for lacking self-discipline; people who suffer from attention deficit disorder struggle with it. Fortunately, many seek and receive help in the form of therapy and assistance. But in cases like

Phil's, where there is no biological source, lack of self-discipline is simply a bad habit. As with many self-defeating behaviors, lack of self-discipline has its roots in how you were raised.

Phil's mother had been ill when he was a child, and a kind of quiet chaos ruled. The house was usually a mess, with dishes left unwashed, beds unmade, and dirty laundry piled up. Whenever guests came, Phil would simply stuff dirty clothes in the closet or literally sweep dirt under the rug.

Often, Phil didn't finish his homework. His teachers would give him time in class to work on it, but quietly resented the fact that his parents seemed so laissez-faire. Living in a world in which self-discipline was not considered a value, Phil did not learn to value it himself. Instead, he learned to scrape by. He got in the habit of waiting until the last minute to do things, and of making excuses for his slipups.

Dan Sullivan, founder of Toronto-based Strategic Coach, offers seminars to help high-performing people gain control of their "out of control" lives. He notes that he rarely hears people use the term "self-discipline" in a constructive way. "Rather than helping people find a solution, it is mostly used by them to beat up on themselves or someone else for a character defect," he says. In his seminars, he "excuses" his audience from lacking self-discipline and insists they no longer use it to describe themselves. He explains: "It's not about lacking self-discipline. It's about habits. Successful people have different habits than unsuccessful people; happy people have different habits than unhappy people." He emphasizes that it takes twenty-one days to replace a bad old habit with a positive new one.

The best way to change habits is to embark on a new, positive one that results in being more effective. This begets feeling more positive. Then, as the saying goes, "success breeds success," and you're on your way instead of being stuck in your own way.

> Repetition of the same thought or physical action
> develops into a habit which, repeated frequently enough,
> becomes an automatic reflex.
>
> —Norman Vincent Peale

PHIL MANAGED to break his old habits in just this way. His boss's remark kicked him in the rear. He thought of what he could do differently and, more important, something that he could do consistently over time so that his boss would see that he *could* change. Over the next several months, Phil made sure to check his work thoroughly before presenting it to his team. He discovered that by finishing his designs a day earlier than usual and then sleeping on it, he could look at what he had produced with fresh eyes and catch the flaws he had overlooked. As his new habit took hold, he found that he had no more reason to complain about his lack of self-discipline or to make excuses.

> An unfortunate thing about this world is that the good
> habits are much easier to give up than the bad ones.
>
> —W. Somerset Maugham

PHIL'S TEAM felt better about him. His boss was relieved. "I want to apologize to you for *never* thinking you had it in you to change," she told him. "You proved me wrong. And you have made me reevaluate some of *my* bad habits that keep me from being the best leader I can be."

>>> Action Steps

1. A great way to get started on the right foot is to enroll the people who are frustrated with your lack of self-discipline in your self-improvement program. Identify who they are and consider them your "stakeholders."

2. Tell your stakeholders that you are seeking to improve yourself and want to start some new habits that will recoup any respect they may have lost for you. Tell them your goal is to make them more eager to work with you.

3. Too soft for your tastes? Want something that will affect the bottom line? Think about this: When you go from ticking people off by being oblivious to them with your bad habits, to being considerate and gracious with your new ones, you will dramatically transform the people who now root against you into rooting for you.

Chapter 10

Wasting Time

> Waste your money and you're only out of
> money, but waste your time and you've lost
> a part of your life.
>
> —Michael Leboeuf

HOW OFTEN DOES A DAY or a week go by with your
feeling you've accomplished very little? How often do you
start a day with the best of intentions only to check the
clock at five P.M. and realize you're not much further along
than when you began at nine A.M.? How much do you beat
up on yourself after you've wasted yet another day? If
these questions speak to you, then maybe it's time to do
things differently.

It's astonishing how many people waste their time at

work. In the February 2002 issue of the *Harvard Business Review*, an article titled "Beware the Busy Manager" revealed the extent of the time-wasting problem. The authors' research showed that a full ninety percent of managers waste their time by procrastinating (see chapter 1, "Procrastinating"), burying themselves in frenetic busywork, or just feeling out of it and disengaged. Only ten percent of the managers they studied truly applied themselves.

Since just about everyone, it seems, wastes time, then why is it a problem? It's like trying to get work done during the week between Christmas and New Year's. No one is around, so why bother working?

On a personal level, it's simply a matter of effectiveness, and I'll say more about this in a minute. If you want to accomplish things at work, you need to focus on efficiency.

Focus is difficult, in part, because the workplace is practically set up to foil it. Distraction and busywork and silly systems are like a swift river, and employees are like so many salmon trying to swim upstream.

Lee Ryan, founder and head of the Los Angeles–based executive search firm Ryan Miller Associates, can't stand institutional time-wasting. Ryan is not a man who suffers fools or foolishness gladly. Since recruiting is essentially about putting the right candidate fit into the right client fit, many firms gather as many candidates as they can and throw them at as many positions as possible in the hope that a few will stick. That process initially involves calling the possible applicants for the job (seventeen, for example, is not an excessive number in the firms that throw candidates at positions). And when the match doesn't work out, it entails a number of time-consuming, not to mention uncomfortable, calls to rejected candidates. A final call is to the company to apologize for sending them the wrong candidates. The total, on average, comes to fifty-one explanatory calls.

"Regardless of your explaining, it's clear to all that you don't really know what you're doing," Ryan says in frustration. "What a colossal waste of time that is. In our business, time is too valuable to waste. Better to take the time to get to know what and who the client company is looking for and then select two or three candidates that are likely to fit. And yet so few companies do that."

> It has been my observation that most people get ahead during the time that others waste.
>
> —Henry Ford

YOU MAY waste time because you are in a *reactive* mode, meaning that you don't make and take time to think. You may also feel that doing more faster will make you more effective. You probably feel like you spend all day at work reacting to stuff—e-mail, documents, requests from bosses and colleagues and clients, and on and on. You probably feel like the little Dutch boy with his thumb in the dike. Time is at such a premium anyway, so how can you possibly take time to think? But the problem is that a reactive approach to work only leads to panic and mistakes. As one client told me, "When as certain as you thought you were is as wrong as you turn out to be, it not only stops you in your tracks; it stops you in your brain. You begin to second-guess yourself about every decision you've made."

Here's the irony, and it is huge: By taking time to think—and by that I mean adopting a *proactive* "measure twice, cut once" strategy to your workday, week, and month—you *save* time because you are more effective and the quality of your work will be better. This means making sure you understand what's most important for you to do, especially when you have people demanding things from you that are important to them. You get better at filtering out the things that are time-wasters. (E-mail, for example, is one of the greatest time-eaters on the planet.)

It's not a matter of setting priorities according to importance, but according to who is going to be most ticked off at you if you don't do it *and do it well*.

> Time is the scarcest resource and unless it is managed
> nothing else can be managed.
>
> —Peter F. Drucker

So how do you take a proactive approach to your work? Ryan recommends thinking ahead of time about the goals you are aiming for and how best to get there. This means taking a few minutes at the beginning and end of each day to devote yourself to the most important tasks—and there should be no more than three each day. Accomplish them, and you will find yourself much more productive.

Usable Insight

It takes much more time to clean up a mess than it does to think ahead and avoid creating one.

⟫⟫ Action Steps

1. Start with a short list (no more than three) of weekly, high-priority goals for yourself. Accomplish these for four weeks; then change to monthly goals.
2. Without editing, list all the ways you can accomplish these goals. This list should include not only what you need to do but what you need to stop doing, who you need something

from, and who to tell you're not going to be available to in order for you to reach your goals.

3.   Don't embark on e-mail and phone calls (unless they are critical) until after you have accomplished one important thing in the morning. Keep "e-mail and phone call hours," as you might office hours.

4.   Practice saying no. If saying no to some people other than your boss is too daunting, select your most "powerful" supervisor or boss to intervene and request that they borrow you away so you can do what your boss wants you to do (see "Fear of Confrontation").

5.   If you find yourself doing more compulsive behaviors—checking e-mail every few minutes, taking long breaks or lunches, being late to work—ask yourself what you are feeling frustrated about that's driving you to distraction. See in your mind's eye what changes in your work situation would quickly lessen your frustration and your need for these diversions. Take a twenty-minute exercise break and get back to work.

6.   Ask your boss to help you achieve better, doable results.

Chapter 11

Thinking You're Indispensable

> A man doesn't begin to attain wisdom
> until he recognizes that he is no longer
> indispensable.
>
> —Richard Byrd

"WE HAVE A SITUATION HERE." That's the opening to a call I received from a senior human resources manager who called me in to help the company disentangle itself from a valued but high-maintenance executive.

The "situation" involved Anthony, who headed the firm's flagship unit that had produced the lion's share of revenues for years. He was charismatic and telegenic—a good public face for the company.

Anthony, recently divorced, was feeling more than his

oats. At a company party, he openly groped one of his staffers in full view of others. It wasn't the first of his public indiscretions, but because he excelled in his job, the people in power tended to overlook them. Still, the groping incident had pushed things over the top. It was clearly a bad move, and people talked. And talked. And talked. And eventually the HR person called me.

Some highly valued employees feel their special abilities allow them to break the rules. But bringing a lot of business into a company—as Anthony did—isn't enough to make up for stepping over people's personal boundaries or ignoring workplace rules in general. Indulging in such behavior undermines the leadership of even the most exalted people. Even though it's commonplace to say "No one is indispensable," too many people have come to believe that they are.

Who are these indispensables? In general, people who are very talented, who've won high praise, or who have a rare skill. Sometimes they are hands-down brilliant. Sometimes they hoard information in an effort to preserve their special status. (I think of this as "the nerd's revenge.")

> The cemeteries are full of indispensable men.
>
> —Charles de Gaulle

OTHER TIMES, the problem is narcissism, which *Webster's* dictionary defines simply as "egotism, egocentrism." All of us can be narcissistic to some degree, but the ones who believe themselves indispensable, like Anthony, tend to come off as larger-than-life personalities.

People who are egotistic, simply put, feel smarter and better than others. Listening only to themselves, they are often deaf to input (see

"Being Closed Off to Input"). Since they are big contributors to their company's bottom line, they're tolerated.

If one or two brave people have told you that you are egotistic or a poor listener, chances are that overcompensation is a big part of your life. You have something to prove to the world—you want to get back at it, you want the world to love you, or you want to conquer it. There is a good chance that you didn't get the love and attention you needed as a child, so as an adult you have grown used to taking without asking. Accordingly you may feel isolated, and while you hear words of admiration, they may roll off your back. You keep pushing the envelope because whatever you receive now is not enough to compensate for what you failed to receive as a child.

How do you get past thinking you are indispensable? Said another way, how do you get over yourself? First of all, you really have to want to. Typically it takes a big slap upside the head for such people to become aware of their problem. Such was the case with Anthony. Used to seeing himself as the hero, he was now the fool. His company fired him on grounds of sexual harassment, and he had trouble finding a job thereafter because word got out about his behavior. Suddenly he had to face up to himself, and the experience was unpleasant. If you think you're indispensable and haven't had your slap upside the head yet, brace yourself—you will sooner or later.

> This is the very perfection of a man, to find out
> his own imperfections.
>
> —Saint Augustine

IF YOU want to succeed, remember that people will root for a reformed jerk more than they will for someone who has been nice all along. When you reform, 20 percent of people will cheer for you out of sincere appreciation; the remaining 80 percent will cheer because they feel such relief at being able to let go of the "fear and loathing" they have felt toward you. Keep up the reform plan, and soon you will begin to inspire people to improve and reform themselves because they'll think that if you can change, so can they. And after that they will do their utmost for you.

Usable Insight

Why get off on driving people to want to kill you, when you could inspire them to want to kill *for* you?

⟫⟫⟫ Action Steps

1. Do a jerkectomy on yourself. Start by writing a list of those irreplaceable things you think you do. Then write a list of people who can do those things. (If you can't come up with a list, you're not being honest with yourself—so try again.)

2. Now ask yourself, "What behaviors am I engaging in that I've been warned about, directly or indirectly?"

3. Think of a beloved person in your life, alive or dead, who is or would be disappointed by your behavior. If you feel ashamed or embarrassed, you're on the right track. Think of the people your behavior has affected and then offer them a sincere apology.

    Find someone who will be frank with you and tell you when you are being a jerk, and then work on breaking the habit.

Chapter 12

People
Pleasing

If you want to be respected by others, the
great thing is to respect yourself. Only by
that, only by self-respect, will you compel
others to respect you.

—Fyodor Dostoyevsky

RAYMOND WORKED for a Los Angeles electrical-
equipment wholesaler when family problems forced the
sales manager to suddenly move out of town. Popular with
customers and his fellow salespeople, Raymond was the
owner's choice to take the vacated position.

But never having been on a managerial track, Raymond
didn't know where to begin. "It was awful," he recalled.

"Rather than upsetting the people who worked for me, I'd let them off the hook, then step in and smooth over the problems. I tried to be liked by everyone, but they walked all over me." Raymond didn't know how to command the respect he needed to hold his employees accountable for their actions. The end result was that he was miserable: He was the boss in name, but nobody treated him like one, and he sure didn't feel like one.

After several months, he got tired of conflicts and began withdrawing into his office. Then, a few salespeople started mouthing off to customers, whose ensuing complaints got back to the owner. Only after Raymond received a harsh lecture did he decide he'd had enough.

Disastrous managerial debuts like this one are common. New managers often err by being either too eager to please and sacrificing control, or too controlling, triggering rebellion. Managing other people for the first time is strange and difficult. But it's not just new managers who get into trouble when they bend over backward to be liked.

People pleasing is a boomerang: The more you try to get people to like you, the less they like you in terms of respecting you. People pleasers are like puppies that demand attention. They're cute at first, but they get irritating if they don't back off. I know a woman who was such a perfect people pleaser that others would actively go out of their way to disturb her equilibrium and engage her anger. When someone made her cry, she asked me, "Why would anyone want to treat me that way?"

"Because you were asking for it," I told her.

> Never esteem anything as of advantage to you that will make you break your word or lose your self-respect.
> —Marcus Aurelius Antoninus

WHY MUST you work so hard to gain the approval of others? Psychologically speaking, the problem is not terribly complicated, though it is terribly misguided for you because you are trying to repair the past. (People who grow up with alcoholics tend to be people pleasers: The syndrome of codependency sets in and takes root in family members who will do anything to keep the peace amid the chaos of living with an alcoholic or in an otherwise dysfunctional household.)

So you crave the positive attention denied you as a child. You probably also discovered that you could manipulate teachers and adults other than parents by being "good" and "kind" and "nice" and "efficient," or whatever your method of choice was. Pleasing people gained you the favor and attention you wanted. It's always worked as a control and coping mechanism—at least in the short run. But in the long run, it's a failure.

Women are especially prone to people pleasing because their connection to their self-worth is directly affected by their relationships ("If I'm liked, I'm worth more; if I'm not liked, I'm worthless"). Conversely, men's connection to their self-worth is more often directly affected by their competence ("If I'm competent, I'm worth more; if I'm not, I'm worthless").

Typically, people pleasers exhibit some or all of the following behaviors. First, they become overachievers, working extremely hard to accomplish the end that gains them praise. Second, they tend to be compulsively (as opposed to calmly) organized in order to lessen the chance that they'll "mess up" figuratively and literally. Third, they placate people in order not to upset them. Fourth, they are outgoing, friendly, gregarious, supportive, creative, happy, encouraging, positive, and cooperative because they think all these things will earn them points. Fifth, they volunteer to work on new projects, accept new assignments, go along with requests, and are considered warm and friendly so people will think well of them.

All good assets, right? Yes and no.

A "no" uttered from the deepest conviction is better
than a "yes" merely uttered to please, or worse,
to avoid trouble.

—Mahatma Gandhi

PEOPLE PLEASING may be a charming seduction technique in children, but carried into adulthood it leads to all kinds of problems. Instead of listening to yourself, you've conditioned yourself to listen to others. You have trouble with boundaries. In your quest for "yes" you find it hard to say "no." You take on too much. You want to be loved so you trust too easily, and as a result you give away your power. You may have even endangered yourself at one time or another. Worst of all, you lose the respect of those whose respect you most crave. Time to stop.

Does this mean you have to stop being nice? Absolutely not. What it does mean is that you need to set up a series of traffic lights—red for stop, yellow for caution, green for go—and filter people through those colors. This means creating a different framework for yourself. Instead of thinking of yourself as a panting puppy yearning for a scratch on the head, think of yourself as the master—a person whose respect you would want.

Masters have boundaries. To become a master you need to build boundaries in order to protect and respect yourself. Think of yourself as that puppy you were, who so needed attention and kindness. That puppy craves not superficial approval but something much deeper—a good master who is kind, who mentors it, who shows it the ropes and loves it but also teaches and enforces the rules.

A good master doesn't let a puppy run into a busy street. Instead, he teaches the puppy to be careful. A good master shows the puppy how to discern fight from flight, good people from bad people, and so on. You are an adult puppy who needs guidance and parenting of a kind but firm master. Now be the master. Build your boundaries. Set rules with yourself.

> Self-empowerment [is] learning to respect other people's music, but dance to your own tune as you master harmony within yourself.
>
> —Doc Childre

AS A RECOVERING people pleaser, you must also teach your inner puppy to say no. If you supervise others, practice delegating (see "Not Delegating"). If you don't supervise others and people ask you to do things that eat up your time but really don't move you forward at work, say no. It's all right. The sky won't fall.

Stop trying to be friends with everyone. You want to be *friendly*, of course, but keep your distance with people at work. This doesn't mean you must stop having lunch with your old buddies after you receive a promotion, but you don't have to be buddies with people just because they work with you. Commanding respect starts with saying no when people are unreasonable. You can be respected or liked, you can lead or not lead. It's up to you.

USABLE INSIGHT

If you sacrifice being respected in order to be liked, you won't be either.

▶▶▶ Action Steps

1. Write down the names of some people at work (a boss, peers) whose increased respect for you would make you more successful.

2. Ask yourself whether they like you more than they respect you. If you decide that you want to increase their respect levels, proceed with the next steps.

3. Identify one specific, observable, and consistent behavior you could adopt toward each of these people that you believe will increase their respect for you.

4. Now ask each person whether the behavior you have chosen would improve your work relationship with them. If not, ask if they can think of an alternative behavior to work on that they think would increase the productivity of your working relationship.

5. If they suggest something you can do, agree to do it. (If they feel awkward, they have the option of agreeing with your suggestion.) Let them know you're going to check in with them periodically to see whether the new behavior is working well or not.

6. Make sure you thank them after this conversation and again a day later.

7. DON'T go through this process unless you are committed to following through.

Chapter 13

Feeling Guilty

Guilt upon conscience, like rust upon iron,
both defiles and consumes it, gnawing and
creeping into it, as that does which at last
eats out the very heart and substance
of the metal.

—Bishop Robert South

"**YOU FIRED EVERYONE** who worked at Universal Studios. Didn't you feel guilty?" I asked Al Dorskind, a former top executive at MCA, after his company purchased Universal Studios many years before. According to Al, the people at Universal were used to making movies. They weren't used to the strict discipline needed to produce television shows. They weren't getting the message, so Al said, "You're fired," to everyone who worked there, and then had them reapply for their jobs.

"I wasn't happy to do it, but I was glad I did it because it saved the studio," he responded.

I was still having trouble with his response, imagining the guilt I would have felt in his position. Sensing my conflict, Al made his position clearer. "Why should I feel guilty? I'm not the one who did something wrong. They weren't performing, and I was responsible for keeping the company alive." He paused and looked keenly at me, reading my thoughts. "Mark, people can feel hurt and it doesn't mean *you've* hurt them."

That last comment of Al's made me realize the distinction between *feeling* guilty and *being* guilty. I also realized what a waste of time feeling guilty can be. When you feel guilty, it eats away at you. You're stuck in a no-win situation.

Consider the case of Deborah, a public relations manager in a large software firm, who handles a staff of five people. When Deborah was promoted, a staffer named Joe was bitter: He felt he was better qualified for the job. Deborah felt guilty for having beaten out Joe for the promotion. This drove her to try to soothe his feelings.

She regularly took Joe out to lunch; she had "check-in" meetings with him; she openly complimented his work to the point that other staffers suspected her of playing favorites.

But Joe saw Deborah's gestures as a mark of managerial weakness and talked about this behind her back. Deborah sensed that Joe had issues, but persisted in believing she could change his attitude. Soon enough, the poisonous employee succeeded in turning the rest of the staff against Deborah, who suffered in her own performance reviews as a result.

I have never smuggled anything in my life. Why, then, do
I feel an uneasy sense of guilt on approaching a customs
barrier?

—John Steinbeck

THERE ARE few self-defeating behaviors that separate effective
leaders from ineffective ones more than feeling guilty. Leading is about
making decisions, often tough decisions, and ones that you need to
stand behind even if they result in people being hurt or disappointed.

Why do some people feel they have done something wrong when
they haven't? If you think about it, those who feel guilty have lovely
motives. They assume responsibility for the hurt and disappointment
of others as if they caused it. They're moved to give something back or
make things right. They feel this way because they cannot tolerate
someone being upset with them.

If you often feel guilty, you probably grew up in a household in
which guilt was a currency (as tends to be the case in many religious
homes). You were doubtless made to feel responsible for another family member's happiness, most likely a parent's. Since you were depend-
ent on your parents, you feared their withdrawal; you would disappoint
them at your own peril.

In time you may have unconsciously decided that guilt was part of
you, as much a part of you as your hands or your eye color. You may also
have realized that guilt is a terrific motivator and that it has paid off for
you in some ways—you may be a perfectionist who received good
grades and high marks from employers, who feels guilty if you don't
achieve what you think you should.

Unfortunately, there is no payoff for guilt. It leaves you feeling sad
and empty and living in regret rather than in the joy you deserve. In

simple terms, guilt is a choice you are making that gets in the way of your own high performance. When you do things out of guilt at work, you can run into all kinds of walls. You may have trouble saying no and so overcommit and feel obligated to do more than you can reasonably handle. You may believe you are performing poorly when you aren't, and spend most of your time trying to shore up your weaknesses rather than playing to your strengths. You may feel slightly paranoid, as if you were living in a glass house. You may obsess about your mistakes.

> Guilt is anger directed at ourselves.
>
> —Peter McWilliams

IF YOU feel guilty when you shouldn't, the key is to draw boundaries between your responsibility and others'.

USABLE INSIGHT

Don't confuse *feeling* guilty with *being* guilty.

》》》 Action Steps

1. Next time you're feeling guilty about an action involving you and someone else, ask yourself:
    - What is the other person's responsibility? What expectation do I have of them? Is my expectation fair and reasonable, given their position and job responsibilities?
    - What is my responsibility? Am I assuming more than I need to or should?

2.   Make a list of all the people in your job who currently cause you to feel guilty and ask the same questions about your role and theirs.

3.   If there is some confusion, don't make false assumptions. Instead, have a conversation with the people you feel guilty about to clarify expectations and responsibilities.

Chapter 14

Not Being Able to Take No for an Answer

> You can tell whether a man is clever by his answers. You can tell a man is wise by his questions.
>
> —Naguib Mahfouz

RECENTLY, someone told me a story about a self-confident consultant who was trying to get in the door with a mid-sized manufacturing firm. The firm scheduled him for an appointment to make his pitch after he had submitted a proposal. The reception was warm, and the consultant thought he had sealed the deal.

But when the firm came back with questions, the consultant grew defensive. Put off by his tone, the executive quietly began looking through the other proposals, then selected the first runner-up.

When he called the consultant to deliver the bad news, the consultant blew up. To him, "no" was a call to war. "How can you possibly hire those guys?" he said of the competitor. "The solution I'm offering is absolutely the right one for your firm," he told a top executive. "I've laid out everything you need to know." He accused the manufacturing firm of acting in bad faith.

In the long run, however, the consultant garnered a reputation for being cocky and uncompromising, and his business suffered as a result.

> Knowledge speaks, but wisdom listens.
>
> —Jimi Hendrix

"No" is certainly hard to take. One of the toughest pieces of news anyone can receive is to be told that they have cancer. The big C, that one-word harbinger of possible death, has a way of cutting through even the strongest denial in both patients and doctors. A patient can come in complaining of a cough; a doctor performs tests; hope reigns. The patient can keep asking, "Will I be okay?" But once the X-rays and tests are in, so is the stark, black-and-white reality that the answer to his hopeful question might be "No, you won't."

As a young psychiatry resident at UCLA, I worked on the oncology ward. As part of my job, I tried to imbue my patients with the philosophy "Hope for the best; plan for the worst." I felt this allowed them the room to work within the ropes, so to speak, by putting their domestic and spiritual houses in order. It also helped me, as a doctor, face the prospect of their survival or death along with them.

Today, I still make calls to terminally ill patients. In their cases, "no" is final. No, there are no options that we know of. No, they won't be "okay." The only choice from here on out is how to deal with the bad news. Some people, like the consultant, flail against it, usually to their own detriment. Others accept it gracefully, make their peace, and move on. I've known many a dying person who broke through the terminal "no" and passed on with remarkable dignity, to the great pride and relief of their families.

The business world, for all its difficulties, is not about life and death: It's about making choices. In work life, as one of my mentors, Dr. Edwin Shneidman, a foremost authority on death and dying, told me, "There is always treatment, and sometimes a cure." In business, the difference between people who can't take no for an answer and those who can is simple. People who are able to deal with "no" have a prepared backup plan. People like the arrogant consultant—or the CEOs of companies like Enron and Worldcom—have no such plan and so have a much harder time of it. This is because they have put all their eggs in one basket; believing they are the best, they never plan for the worst.

But if you have a backup plan, are you already setting yourself up for the possibility of defeat? Are you being too negative? The short answer is no. It's merely realistic. The consultant might have found ways of making a deal with the manufacturing firm, short of getting everything he wanted. He could have listened, compromised, and constructed a win-win. Instead, he chose to view the deal as a fight and a zero-sum game: In order to win, he believed the competition had to lose.

For some people, hearing no isn't a defeat; it's an invitation to turn a negative into a positive. But doing this doesn't mean fighting back; it means being clever and listening respectfully to the other side. Consider the case of Walter Dunn, a tremendously wise and successful former executive VP at Coca-Cola who worked for many years with the company's esteemed former president Donald Keough.

Walter was pursuing an account with one of the largest chains of movie theaters. After much time and effort, the account manager from the theater chain told Walter, "I'm sorry, but we have decided to go with Pepsi."

Disappointed but undeterred, Walter replied, "What questions did I fail to ask, or what concerns did I fail to address that affected your decision?"

The theater chain manager replied, "Well, Pepsi offered to help finance a new campaign to renovate our theaters. You might have had the account had you asked about the renovations we were planning and found a creative way to help us with that."

Without missing a beat, Walter replied, "We can still do *that.*" Coca-Cola developed a comarketing plan with the theaters, threw in some money to help fund the renovations, and received the account.

> The world changed from having the determinism of a
> clock to having the contingency of a pinball machine.
> —Heinz Pagels

WALTER'S BACKUP plan consisted of four elements. First, he asked a smart "listening" question. Instead of being defensive, he asked for an elucidating opening. Second, he didn't get belligerent or act hurt. By demonstrating poise, he earned the theater manager's respect. Third, he used that respect to gain another opening.

Finally, Walter understood that helping the theater manager come up with a strong alternative to take back to his boss would help the manager look good. Walter showed that it's how you respond to no that really matters.

The better your contingency plan, the more poise you have when someone says no. The more poise you show, the greater the chance they'll then say yes to you about something.

Usable Insight

The better your backup plan, the easier it will be to take "no" for an answer.

⟫⟫⟫ Action Steps

1. Think of the last time you asked someone for something. How did you react?
2. If you reacted badly, think of two backup plans and different responses that could have helped you turn things around.
3. Now put yourself in the other person's shoes at the time. What valuable offer could you have given them that would have turned things around?
4. How will you prepare yourself for your next "no"?

Chapter 15

Not Forgiving

There is no revenge so complete as forgiveness.

—Josh Billings

IT WAS THE WORST possible way to say good-bye to an otherwise good job. Arlene, an accounting manager at a manufacturing firm with seven years under her belt, had "finally" stood up to her boss, the chief financial officer, in a meeting. She declared out loud, before the whole department, that she could no longer work for him, or for a company that failed to enforce rules against sexual harassment.

Shaken but proud, she walked out of the room and back to her desk. Within five minutes, two security guards and the human resources director showed up, handed her a box, and told her to pack up her personal effects while they stood by and watched, and her teammates whispered and stood in the aisles, observing. Then they took her passkey and escorted her downstairs and out the front door before dozens of whispering, shocked-looking employees who'd peeped from their cubicles to see what was going on.

Arlene was not only embarrassed—she was furious. The unceremonious "escort" only fueled her anger. The first thing she did was to call a reporter at the local newspaper and offer details of her complaint. Then she called her lawyer. She swore she'd "get revenge, no matter how long it takes." (No, she didn't go on a shooting spree; tragically, many others who feel wronged by their employers have done so.)

Now it's three years after the fact, and Arlene—a single mother of two—is still eaten up with anger and frustration over treatment she felt was biased, unfair, and downright hostile, especially in the face of her years of devoted service. Her anger has infected her world to the extent that her children suffer from it, for a parent so distracted by negative emotion is an absent parent.

Letting go of the past is hard for everyone. Little rudenesses (getting cut off in traffic, for example) irk us—but most of us don't fall into road rage. Massive hurts, on the other hand, can wound us for a lifetime if we let them. I've seen people who go through divorces refuse to get over it, nursing anger as if it were a gin and tonic.

On the other hand, I think of people who have to look in the eyes of the murderers of their children, and I shudder. How do they do that? Amazingly, they call on forgiveness. They know they have to move on if they are to make any sense of the rest of their lives. How I admire them.

When bad things happen to you at work, the feelings of embarrassment, grief, rage, and frustration are just as wounding, though they are on a different scale and in a different dimension. I'm not implying that

Arlene should have put up and shut up—far from it. But dealing with the fallout was more under her control than she realized.

> The weak can never forgive. Forgiveness is the attribute of the strong.
>
> —Mahatma Gandhi

CERTAINLY, the workplace is full of wrongdoing—from misaligned corporate policies, to greedy executives, to questionable agendas, to collegial nastiness. Most people find a way to negotiate the slings and arrows of workplace indignities in the name of a paycheck (which of course creates its own set of problems). Fortunately, most companies offer some recourse for workers who feel they have been treated unjustly, and some balance is brought to the table before too much destruction occurs. The difference between an Arlene and a more successful worker is that the successful one doesn't need to feel wounded, and so can find more objective ways of dealing with problems.

So why do you hang onto your anger? Frankly, *you get a kick out of it.* Anger feels empowering because you "get" to feel wronged. Not forgiving is an identity. Being wronged is a core part of who you "are." Anger lets you shut out dialogue and alternate views just as effectively as if you were putting a headset on your ears and filling them with a loud CD full of self-righteousness. Bitterness bolsters your sense of yourself as "right." Being right just feels weirdly good.

And I'm sorry to say this, but failing to forgive is also a surefire, fast boomerang that only hurts you. For every moment you focus on the people who hurt you, you overlook the people who care about you.

Every time you fail to appreciate and acknowledge the good people in your life, the bad people win.

Arlene, for example, is now working at a job for which she is far overqualified at half her former salary. The lawsuit is grinding on with no end in sight, and she's used up her life savings in lawyer's fees. Her old boss is still in power at the company, and no additional complaints of harassment have been reported. When a few former colleagues called to ask how she was doing, Arlene launched into a long and bitter rant that both surprised and alienated them (see "Confusing Dumping with Venting"). After all, they hadn't left their jobs, and it happened a long time ago. So they dropped her.

Unforgivingness is the hurt that keeps on hurting. If you let it go, you wouldn't know what to do with yourself, so integrated is your anger into the fabric of your being. Chances are you've lost weeks or months or years of your life because of your beloved anger. What a waste of a good life!

If you want to be successful, start by freeing yourself. Here's the irony: *Forgiving has nothing to do with those you're forgiving. It's all about freeing yourself.* If you want to move on and be prosperous and successful in your life, get over it.

> To forgive, we need to spit out the hook.
> —Dr. Ed Hallowell

THE CORE of forgiveness comes from understanding the position of the person you perceive to be your enemy. Most probably, the person had the same self-sabotaging instincts as you. Empathize with the other person by asking and answering, "Why did he do what he did?" You will make the fascinating and liberating discovery that you can't genuinely put yourself in other people's shoes and be angry with them at the same time. That is because when you are seeking to understand, you are first taking in information with your senses and then processing it with the higher part of your mind; when you are not forgiving (that is, holding on to your anger), you are retaliating against them for some perceived assault or affront to you via the "motor," or reactive, part of your mind.

It's not as hard as you think, but it takes practice. Ritual is a wonderful way to forgive, and it works. The action steps below will work if you practice them.

USABLE INSIGHT

If you look for reasons to forgive you can always find them; if you look for reasons not to forgive you can always find them, too. It comes down to what you *want* to look for.

>>> Action Steps

1. Think of the person(s) whom you cannot forgive. Rate on a scale of 1 to 10 how angry you still are with them (where 1 = not at all, and 10 = wishing an anvil would fall from some height on their heads).

2. Ask yourself, "Why did they do what they did, when they did it?" Answer by filling in the blank: "They did what they did because _____, and they did it when they did because _____."

3. Unless they are truly evil, you will most likely discover that what they did was more their way of coping with something than their assaulting you for no reason.

4.   After you answer the questions above, rate your anger with them (using the 1 to 10 scale). Your anger should have decreased.

5.   If it is lower, ask yourself whether (a) you want to lower it more, or (b) you'd prefer to go back to being angry at them. If you answered (a), continue to look for additional things about them with which to empathize. If you answered (b), there is more of a possibility that you are "unforgiving" than that they are unforgivable. Don't go down that road, for you will spend your life in bitterness.

6.   Renounce your anger *out loud*. Anger can be a demon that takes total control over you. You want your life back.

Chapter 16

Panicking

> You can conquer almost any fear if you will
> only make up your mind to do so. For
> remember, fear doesn't exist anywhere
> except in the mind.
>
> — Dale Carnegie

BOB ECKERT, the CEO of Mattel, Inc., told me the story of a time when panic nearly overtook him. It was a Sunday afternoon in 1990, and the thirty-five-year-old Eckert, then a division president at Kraft Foods, stared at an NFL game on television. He felt like a deer in the headlights of a career disaster.

The *Chicago Tribune* had accused Kraft of price gouging. The outcries against the company and Eckert were immediate and strong. "Legislators were talking about coming down on Kraft as a monopoly, and multiple trade rags said that heads were going to roll," he recalled. "And the head that would roll first would no doubt be mine. My fear was palpable." Watching the game, he felt like he was about to be massively and injuriously tackled.

Bob's experience is hardly unique. Anyone who has felt an overwhelming sense of impending doom knows what Bob was experiencing. You feel like you're standing on thin ice in the middle of a pond and hearing a terrifying "crack." You're frozen in a damned-if-you-do, damned-if-you-don't state, waiting to drown in dark ice water.

What happens to you when you feel so afraid? As your imagination has its field day, the sudden flood of "fight or flight" adrenaline jacks up your heart rate and blood pressure. Your brain is literally hijacked by the chemistry of fear. It starts looking for things to be afraid of to match the physiological response you are having. "Feeling" is believing: Your body is making you feel things that aren't real. And you feel in danger regardless of what anyone tells you. When this happens, you become tense, grumpy, and overly sensitive, and you have trouble focusing and making decisions.

> What are fears but voices airy?
> Whispering harm where harm is not.
> —William Wordsworth

HOW DO YOU get a grip on yourself and escape from the cycle of panic? The key is to put your rational mind back in control. First, you must say to yourself (protectively but firmly), "Just because you feel frightened, doesn't mean you are in any danger. Stop thinking what you're thinking."

To stop the cycle of panic, take some behavioral action that breaks the adhesions that seem to be gripping you. Take several deep, slow breaths through your nose with your eyes closed. (Interestingly, just doing that will cause most people to experience a change in consciousness.) Pick some very ordinary, routine task that refocuses your brain. You might try doing a short crossword puzzle, for instance. (It's also helpful to get some exercise—go out for a twenty-minute brisk walk, for example. Exercise has a wonderful mind-clearing effect.) Then pick up and get back to work by continuing to do something routine—editing a memo, making a phone call—that will keep your mind in neutral gear.

Once you're calmer, do something that is challenging but not frightening—something that makes you feel like you have accomplished an important task. The reason for this is twofold. First of all, doing something challenging rewires your brain to prove to you that just because you are scared stiff doesn't mean you can't move. Second, doing something for which you can claim positive responsibility in the face of tremendous fear is one of the greatest self-esteem boosters there is.

> Action is a great restorer and builder of confidence.
> Inaction is not only the result, but the cause, of fear.
> Perhaps the action you take will be successful; perhaps
> different action or adjustments will have to follow. But
> any action is better than no action at all.
> —Norman Vincent Peale

WHEN THE calamity you were so dreading doesn't happen and the crisis passes and you realize that you not only survived, but did something positive and constructive, you can't help but feel positive about yourself.

Bob Eckert did just that, taking his cue from the fiery, innovative Cincinnati Bengals coach Sam Wyche, whom he was watching on that fateful Sunday. The Bengals—who had won the Super Bowl two years earlier—had just lost their ninth game of the season. Wyche had been called on the carpet; it was common knowledge that he was about to lose his job.

A reporter approached him and said, "Coach, you're going to get fired on Tuesday. Tell me about it." Wyche responded directly to the camera: "*You* know I'm going to get fired Tuesday and *I* know. But that's not important. What is important is to help this team get better, up until I'm let go."

Eckert felt stunned. "It seemed like he was talking directly to me," he said. The next morning, he went back to work accepting that he would be fired, but determined to help the company do better in the meantime. Instead of continuing to feel like Chicken Little worrying about the sky falling, he applied himself to important tasks that pulled Kraft through the crisis.

Needless to say, Eckert wasn't fired. He stayed on at Kraft, became its president and CEO, and moved on to the top job at Mattel.

"Of all the advice I've ever received and followed, Wyche's is preeminent," Eckert told me later. "Maybe it's because when you're alone in self-doubt it can escalate rapidly until you can't move. But when someone who's in the hot seat shows such determination, it can inspire you to develop your own resolve. Wyche's advice helped me to overcome being afraid to fail. It guides me still."

USABLE INSIGHT

When you focus on what needs to be done today and then just do it, you stop being afraid of what *might* happen tomorrow.

⟫⟫⟫ Action Steps

1. Next time you're feeling panicked on the job, say to yourself, "You just dumped a bunch of adrenaline into your bloodstream, your pulse and your blood pressure have shot up. Your body, not your brain, is running the show so you think you're in danger. And you're probably not." Now, stop whatever you're doing, get up out of your chair, and take a fast walk outside or up and down the stairs. Take control of the monkey chatter in your brain by doing something mundane, routine, and emotionally neutral.

2. When you feel calmer, ask yourself, "What are the facts of this situation and what about them is convincing me that something bad will happen?"

3. Then say to yourself, "Just let time pass."

4. When you feel calmer still, ask yourself, "What do I need to get done right now?" When you figure that out, go and do it.

Chapter 17

Quitting Too Soon

Most of the important things in the world
have been accomplished by people who have
kept on trying when there seemed to be
no hope at all.

—Dale Carnegie

LEWIS WAS A TALENTED, intelligent, and charming man. Trained as an artist, he was also a very good salesman. He had the gift of gab; his mother often fondly said of him that "he could sell his grandmother her teeth."

Whenever anyone hired him for a job—at a graphic design firm, a bank, an art store, a school—it was love at first sight. He'd enthusiastically go to work, make friends, and succeed fast. His bosses were enthralled, and Lewis seemed happy. But within a few weeks or months, things would start to go wrong. He'd come home and complain to his wife that the bosses mismanaged the company, or that someone was a slack who forced him to do double duty. The complaining grew worse and worse; inevitably, he would come home to announce to his wife that he had quit.

Over the course of a fourteen-year marriage, Lewis proved himself unable to hold down a job. His résumé was spotty and all over the map; he was unable to procure good, reliable references. Eventually his long-suffering wife, who had carried the financial burden for so long, threw in the towel, divorced him, and moved with their child to another state. Lewis had sacrificed his whole life to his habit of quitting too soon.

> You are not obligated to win. You are obligated
> to keep trying to do the best you can every day.
> —Marian Wright Edelman

IT WAS never clear to Lewis's wife exactly why he was a quitter; at first she suspected he was bored; then she thought he was spoiled—especially since she earned most of the money. But in a therapy session she realized he suffered from a deeper problem—the problem of what famed psychologist Martin Seligman identified as "learned helplessness."

As a child, Lewis had been coddled by his mother and grandparents. Instead of being taught to stand up, fall down, and stand up again (see "Why We Get in Our Own Way" in the introduction), he was taught that if he fell down, he would be scooped up. As a result, Lewis never learned what it takes to succeed. He felt inadequate, and helpless to move forward. It's no wonder he chose for a mate a woman who was a child of an alcoholic, for she herself had spent her childhood enabling her drunken father and smoothing things over for her dysfunctional family. (Couples are often attracted by each other's neuroses.)

Now, there's a big difference between quitting too soon and cutting your losses (see "Staying Too Long in a Job You Should Leave"). When you cut your losses, you're making a sensible decision to leave something after you've given it an honest college try and you must stop in order to save yourself. But when you quit too soon, you're operating from fear of assuming responsibility. You may fear success; you may feel like you don't have what it takes to see things through.

It's also important to remember that work—all work—is a means to an end. Lewis failed to understand that his working was part of the marriage contract. Even if he didn't like or was bored by his work, he had a responsibility to his family to keep money coming in. He allowed his own temporary feelings to override the most important thing in his life.

Quitting too soon is a dangerous thing. Lewis took to heart the old saying that "if you can't stand the heat, get out of the kitchen." He didn't understand that by fleeing the kitchen as soon as things got warm, his life would end up half baked.

> People of mediocre ability sometimes achieve outstanding success because they don't know when to quit. Most men succeed because they are determined to.
>
> —George Allen

Usable Insight
You have more control over trying or quitting than you do over succeeding or failing.

---

1. Think of the last time you quit a job and review the positive and negative consequences of having done so.

2. Look at your present situation and write down the potential pluses and minuses of quitting at this time.

3. Make a list of your other options, with the pluses and minuses of each one.

4. Enlist the help of someone who can be objective and nonjudgmental in helping you evaluate the situation. (You might want to go through the previous two steps with that person.)

5. If you are inclined to quit, ask yourself why and why now. Are the reasons justifiable, or are you merely hoping to avoid something unpleasant, such as embarrassment or boredom?

6. If you decide to hang in there, enlist the help and support of someone you can count on.

Chapter 18

Using
Jargon

You can't write about people out of
textbooks, and you can't use jargon. You have
to speak clearly and simply and purely in a
language that a six-year-old child can
understand; and yet have the meanings and
the overtones of language, and the implica-
tions, that appeal to the highest intelligence.
—Katherine Anne Porter

IN 1995, when I served as an adviser to the prosecution
in the infamous murder trial of O. J. Simpson, I saw just
how much damage the use of jargon can do. The prosecution intended to introduce DNA evidence purportedly
taken from the murder scene, Simpson's Ford Bronco, and

his gloves, and proceeded to go into a lengthy scientific description of DNA. Terms like "alleles," "markers," and "titers" were hurled about the courtroom with much sound and fury, clarifying nothing.

One of Dominick Dunne's *Vanity Fair* articles on the trial quoted me as saying, "Although jurors and the media start off each day like a group of Bambis, gamely making their way through the forest of DNA evidence, they end each day looking like deer in the headlights of the *Encylopædia Britannica*."

I clearly recall the expressions on the jurors' faces as the prosecution went into the scientific details surrounding the evidence. Some bit their lips and looked confused, but most knit their brows and nodded, intently doing their best to take it all in, or at the very least to stay awake. It was pretty clear to me that they were confused by the unfamiliar and complex scientific terminology. The prosecution did their best to make it more understandable but the defense's Johnnie Cochran trumped them when he dramatically held up the infamous "bloody glove" and used the simple phrase, "If it doesn't fit, you must acquit." Simplicity won the day.

I'm not offering my opinion regarding the outcome of the Simpson case. On the other hand, I'm convinced that the use of jargon turns people off much more than it impresses or influences them.

jar·gon: (jär'gən) *n.*
1. Nonsensical, incoherent, or meaningless talk.
2. A hybrid language or dialect; a pidgin.
3. The specialized or technical language of a trade, profession, or similar group.
4. Speech or writing having unusual or pretentious vocabulary, convoluted phrasing, and vague meaning.

—American Heritage Dictionary of the English Language

JARGON IS not communication: it's intimidation. I'm not talking about dialect, which is the language people in a region or a group (think of Louisianans or urban adolescents) use when they speak with one another; nor am I talking about the kind of specialized language that people in certain professions—paramedics, for example—must use in very specific situations.

The most malevolent jargon is language that one person deliberately uses either to intimidate or to hide the truth and pull the wool over the eyes of another person. Jargon is a tool many people use to separate innocent folks from their money (car mechanics, technical salespeople, lawyers, doctors, and business consultants can fall into this category, providing verbal fodder for the myriad of "investigative" prime-time TV magazine shows).

> Incomprehensible jargon is the hallmark of a profession.
> —Kingman Brewster

NOT EVERYONE uses jargon malevolently, of course; for many, jargon is a professional hazard. Academics and doctors, for example, have straight talk trained out of them.

I observed the most poignant example of this when I was a third-year medical student doing my oncology rotation at the Boston Veterans Hospital in an episode that started me down the road to becoming a psychiatrist. We were doing rounds in which oncology, surgery, and radiology fellows, medical residents, interns, and medical students would discuss patients' conditions, often in the patients' rooms.

I remember when we discussed a certain Mr. Ackerson's case at his bedside, talking over him as if he weren't there. The oncologist thought he needed more chemotherapy. The radiologist thought we should go with radiation. The surgeon said he needed surgery. Each made his case, using terms specific to his field of expertise. They were all talking over one another. Then we all left.

The next day, as we entered Mr. Ackerson's room, again debating his condition, a nurse interrupted us and said, "Didn't you hear? Mr. Ackerson jumped from the roof last night. He's in the morgue."

Everyone went silent. Clearly, Mr. Ackerson needed much more than jargon.

People in all kinds of professions develop a habit of insider-speak, forgetting that the rest of us don't understand what they're talking about. Information technologists, for example, routinely exchange communication for jargon, which explains why most companies see their IT people as a breed apart. Common technology terms ("WiFi," "open systems," "dot-net," and so on) mystify nontechnical people, who simply want to get their jobs done. The technical jargon understood by IT people—and swapped with a kind of locker-room swagger at technology conferences—is a foreign language to the rest of us, but no one wants to appear foolish by asking for a translation.

Jargon doesn't have to consist of multisyllabic words, by the way; it can also consist of unclear language. CEOs use this kind of jargon all the time. They talk about their companies' "mission," "culture," "vision," and "values" without any precision, with the result that employees have no real sense of direction even as they nod in false agreement.

Where does the urge to use jargon come from? Fundamentally, jargon is all about preserving a false sense of authority; you use it when you're afraid that people will find you out. Moreover, we all tend to collude in other people's jargon for fear of looking stupid. But this doesn't give you or anyone else the right to run over people with our linguistic trucks.

⫸ Action Steps

1. Watch the body language of your listener. Jargon is a way of talking over or at others (see "Talking Over or At Others"). Your listener will try to pretend he or she understands you by saying "uh-huh" in a tone of false comprehension. You might notice that they physically pull away slightly.

2. Rather than asking people if they have any questions (most people will politely respond no, even when they do), ask them to tell you what they understand from what you've said. It may try your patience, but will save you time later when you discover they didn't take in what you thought they had (see "Assuming Others Understand You").

3. Monitor results. If superiors, subordinates, and peers don't respond with the results you expect, they may not be comprehending what you are telling them. Check in by saying, "I'm guessing that what I said might have been unclear." A tone of humility will go a long way here; people will respect your effort.

4. Develop a buddy system with others who speak Jargonese and would also like to improve their communication. Take them aside and tell them you are working to remove unnecessary jargon and you get a sense that they are trying to do the same. Ask them if they would be willing to point out to you when you use it and tell them that you'll do the same for them.

Chapter 19

Worrying About What Others Think

Worry a little bit every day and in a lifetime you will lose a couple of years. If something is wrong, fix it if you can. But train yourself not to worry. Worry never fixes anything.
—Mary Hemingway

ARMED WITH A FRESH bachelor's degree and a paralegal certificate, twenty-three-year-old Fanya was delighted to have landed a job with a large law practice—a move that she thought would help her get into a good law school. Enthusiastic and anxious to prove herself, she dove into her work headlong. When she presented her boss with the results of her first research project, she wasn't sure how he would respond, but she hoped for the best.

When he told her, as neutrally and objectively as possible, that her research had taken a wrong turn and suggested that she start over from another angle, he assumed that she would take it in stride and try again. But for Fanya, the comment was like a body blow. Her self-confidence crumbled. She grew quiet and self-conscious.

Poor Fanya. Smart as she was, she was extremely vulnerable to the imagined feelings of others. She entered a state psychologists refer to as "hypervigilance." Her boss's tone of voice began to sound demeaning. It seemed as if her peers grouped into little cliques that shut her out.

"After John criticized my work, I felt like people were looking at me," Fanya told me. "They'd get together with their friends and gossip behind closed doors. I started to get really paranoid." Feeling uncertain about her decisions and her work, she actually created a self-fulfilling prophecy. The more apprehensive and sensitive she grew, the worse her quality of work became—to the point where her boss really did begin to question whether she was up to the job.

At the root of Fanya's experience was a complex but not uncommon unconscious response that so many of us have to our work "family." In this case, she was transferring feelings about her father to her boss, and about her past schoolmates to her peers (see "Why We Get in Our Own Way" in the introduction).

Fanya grew up with a competitive, critical, and hard-to-please father whose attention and affection she craved. No matter how hard she tried, it seemed, Fanya could not win more than grudging approval. If she brought home an all-but-perfect report card, he would grill her about the B rather than praise her for the A's she'd slaved to earn. Accordingly, Fanya grew up perpetually feeling as if she had done something wrong, when in fact she'd done just about everything right. Because she excelled in school, teachers praised her, but their acceptance mattered less to her than that of the older, popular, good-looking, and athletic kids who dismissed her as an "egghead."

> Honest criticism is hard to take, particularly from a
> relative, a friend, an acquaintance, or a stranger.
>
> —Franklin Jones

CHILDREN WHO grow up with parents who can't or won't listen to them for a variety of reasons (self-obsession, depression, alchoholism, and so on) are dogged by feelings of shame (i.e., "I must not be worth listening to") and incompetence. They internalize their parent's negativity or neglect as a response to their not feeling worthy of anything more. Powerful as they are, such feelings have little to do with the facts. They can and must be mastered—for if we focus on others' real or imagined impressions, we can easily reach a state of mind that seriously interferes with our job performance.

> I was always looking outside myself for strength and
> confidence, but it comes from within. It is there all
> the time.
>
> —Anna Freud

FANYA TOLD ME that she never felt she was good enough because her father never felt *he* was good enough. She heard the echoes of his social rejection in her head, and felt shamed.

To cut the "what are they saying about me" tape, you need to detach yourself from the negative feelings you have and place the experience in a different light. In short, you need to objectify the situation by separating the facts from your feelings. There are four ways to do this:

1. Understand that work is not about who you are; it's about the results you produce. Fanya's boss didn't care about anything

but her ability to deliver a solid research report; his criticism had nothing to do with her personally. In fact, all any boss really cares about is that you will do what you say you will do.

2. Realize that when you are focusing on what you're supposed to be doing, you have nothing to be ashamed or afraid of.

3. Recognize the catch-22. The less confidence you have, the easier it is to be distracted by what you imagine people think of you. The more distracted you become, the less confidence you develop. To escape the catch-22, focus on gaining confidence through doing rather than worrying.

4. Gain confidence by honing your expertise. All of us are better at something than our peers. By identifying a skill or area of knowledge that you bring to the table—perhaps the one that got you the job in the first place—and refining it to the point of expertise, you become more valuable to your organization, while gaining the self-confidence you need to stand your ground. Knowing that you are highly skilled at something is very helpful in keeping your perspective when you think you are incompetent everywhere.

USABLE INSIGHT

Don't confuse feelings with facts.

▶▶▶ Action Steps

1. *Resist discounting yourself.* Whenever you do something well, take time to give yourself credit for being competent. When you find yourself starting to diminish yourself, say, "Stop it! You did well! Don't do that to yourself!" It may help to imagine

a person who believes in and cares about you stepping in to give you praise.

2. *If you make a mistake, don't beat yourself up.* Instead, recognize that no one is perfect. Ask yourself what you might have done differently if you had the opportunity to try the same thing again. Write down your answer.

3. *Avoid office gossip.* Excuse yourself gracefully from invitations to gossip by saying something like, "I'm sorry, but this issue is distracting to me. I hope you'll excuse me."

4. *List all the situations that raise a red flag of fear for you*—facing a performance review, asking for help, and so on. Tell yourself to hope for the best, but remain calm if you receive an upsetting response.

5. *Don't become defensive.* If you are told something about you that is upsetting, don't get into a debate or "Yes, but . . ." conversation. Instead ask, "Going forward, what would you recommend I do differently?" (see "Getting Defensive").

6. *Thank them for their input.* Realize that your boss is more concerned with something being corrected than in punishing you.

Chapter 20

Fear of Learning
New Things

I was afraid of the Internet . . . because I couldn't type.

—Jack Welch

LONG AFTER I GAVE UP trying to keep my hand-written daily planner straight, I knew I needed a personal digital assistant (PDA). But I kept putting off the purchase. Why? I had this fixed notion that I couldn't learn the graffiti handwriting. Then I bought the thing and waited. And waited. With one day left on the fourteen-day return policy, I still hadn't taken it out of the box. Finally I dove into the daunting task. Guess what? I was proficient in graffiti within fifteen minutes. Fifteen minutes! Yet I had put off learning something new for months.

It's one thing to resist getting the hang of a PDA. It's quite another to allow fear of learning, or more precisely fear that you can't learn, to get in the way of career success. In the introduction I told the story of John, the accountant who feared he hadn't learned anything new in ten years and fought a losing battle against change at his company. The world is full of people like John—people who are plenty smart, but who work themselves into irrelevance as their skills are outpaced by the changing world around them.

At work, you might seize up at the prospect of having to learn a new computer skill, a new set of workplace processes, dealing with a new boss. Paradoxically, the more you worry about change, the harder it gets to make the change.

Once upon a time, learning a specific set of skills or holding a college or professional degree was the key to the workplace kingdom. Think of all those people with computer science and engineering degrees: During the height of the high-tech boom, people with technical skills were being snapped up as fast as they could sign their names. And just as fast, the bust came. Many of those people lost their jobs and are having a hard time finding new ones. They're told to go back to school, to learn new skills. But it's not easy, particularly for older workers.

What's going on here? One problem may be lack of time. The more things you learn, the more you may feel you have to hold on to. Your mind may already feel overcrowded; you don't have the mental energy or space to learn new things. With the world spinning faster and faster and the difficulty of retaining information, resistance to change is completely understandable. After all, faster isn't necessarily better, and sometimes we just want the onslaught to stop. It seems more comfortable to not even start the process.

> How do you eat an elephant? One bite at a time.
>
> —Hindu saying

A DEEPER PROBLEM has to do with your lack of confidence in your ability to learn at all. Unless you continually learn in life, fear overtakes your confidence that you *can* learn. I see it all the time in women whose eyes glaze over when they have to do something mathematical—thanks to teachers and parents who brainwashed them into falsely believing they weren't good at math. I see it in men who, convinced that they are nerds, hide in corners at cocktail parties when they're supposed to be schmoozing with clients. It's actually not a case of not being able to learn, but rather of becoming frozen when faced with something new and unfamiliar.

Another block has to do with your comfort level, which is closely allied with your sense of personal identity. Learning a new skill is scary because it demands both effort and that you broaden your image of yourself. Over time, we humans become convinced that we "are" a certain way, and that the way we "are" is written in stone. We even defend being who we think we "are." Over time, we calcify. We may feel we deserve to coast along on our merits. I think of old college professors who keep teaching the same thing year after year and long past their prime. (They have tenure to protect them; the rest of us don't.) Or I think of the grandpa who might go online so he can communicate by e-mail with his favorite grandchild, but who steadfastly refuses to learn about computers, saying he's fine with doing things the old way.

Ironically, the more we believe that we are unable to learn, the more unable to learn we become.

> We now accept the fact that learning is a lifelong process of keeping abreast of change. And the most pressing task is to teach people how to learn.
>
> —Peter Drucker

LEARNING A NEW skill is tough, but if you reframe the situation, it can be challenging and exhilarating. The trick is to tap into a memory of a time when you did learn something new. If you can clearly visualize the experience—say, learning to ski or to drive, learning to use a computer, learning to read music—and recall the memory of conquering the task, then you may be able to trigger the sense of pleasure that came from the experience. If you don't get ahead of yourself thinking of everything you won't be able to learn, and instead focus on what you *have already* learned that you thought you couldn't, your fears will dissipate, your mind will unlock, and you will learn new things.

> Give a man a fish, you feed him for a day; teach a man
> to fish, you feed him for a lifetime; But teach a man to
> learn, you feed him for a lifetime, and he doesn't
> have to just eat fish.
>
> —Tim Gallwey

USABLE INSIGHT

Just because you think you can't learn new things, doesn't mean you can't.

>>> Action Steps

1.   When facing a situation where you think you can't learn something, pause and think of three times in your life when you were convinced you couldn't learn something but did.

2. Remember what tools, assistance (a teacher, a friend, a course), and strategies you employed to learn those new skills.

3. Now remember what the steps were that you took in order to learn. What did you do first? What did you do after that?

4. Now draw a parallel between that memory and the steps you might take to learn what you need to learn now. (For instance, if you recalled learning to drive with an instructor, think of getting an instructor to help you "drive" your new task.)

5. Make a commitment to continuously learn new skills so that you don't become so incapacitated by fear when you have to learn something in the future.

Chapter 21

Being Too Blunt

"Oh, forgive my bluntness. It's a device that I use to cope."

—Elaine, from *Ally McBeal*

A FAMOUS STORY about Winston Churchill goes something like this: Churchill was at a royal garden party, feeling no pain, when a self-righteous old woman noted his condition and exclaimed disapprovingly, "You, sir, are drunk!"

"And you, madam, are ugly," Churchill responded. "But tomorrow, I shall be sober."

Churchill's blunt retort makes us laugh at the equally blunt old woman. Comedians like Robin Williams, Margaret Cho, and John Mayer make their living being blunt.

They are entertaining truth-tellers. When comedians take aim at specific people, groups, or society at large, they say things that most of us may have thought but are either too polite or politically correct to say out loud and in public. We laugh at their bluntness in part because we know there's no way we could do what they do. We admire their raw nerve, and reward them with applause.

At work, some people get a thrill out of saying things that the rest of us would consider impolitic. Sometimes their comments are funny; sometimes they're not. Most often bluntness is a cry for attention.

Consider the case of Lucy, fresh from business school, who had just taken a job at a large financial services firm in Boston. As a newbie and one of the relatively few female financial analysts, she was in an environment that was not comfortable for her. She felt judged by the men in the firm—particularly by her boss—who liked her freshness but also expected her to compete toe to toe with others "like a guy." When she asserted herself in meetings, the men around her appeared to either discount what she said or ignore her altogether.

> Don't confuse being stimulating with being blunt.
> —Barbara Walters

LUCY DID not like feeling ignored. So she reverted to a habit she'd developed in early adolescence: being blunt. The sixth of seven children in a household in which both parents worked, Lucy had to fight to get noticed. Consumed by feelings of anxiety, Lucy felt like a tire with a slow leak—she had to keep pumped up to feel alive. So she became a drama queen, inflating herself by impulsively saying what others wouldn't. She discovered that by saying funny or outrageous things, she could get her distracted parents and plethora of siblings to notice her. If Lucy happened to let loose in a social situation, her mother would try to laugh it off. "Oh, that Lucy," her mother would say. "She's just so honest! She can't help herself."

At the firm, Lucy grasped for attention by commenting acerbically on the behavior of her colleagues. In one meeting, she interrupted a long-winded fellow who had launched into what she thought was a tedious explanation by saying, "George, let's just cut to the chase, shall we?" One time in the lunchroom, she declared another colleague to be a "zero." When her boss suggested that she try to be a little more discreet in her opinions, Lucy became defensive. "Look, I call things as I see them," she said. "It's obvious that George talks too much. And everyone knows Joe's lights aren't all on. I'm just the only one who says it."

Lucy thought she was just being forthright. But her boss felt Lucy's sharp tongue was a liability, so he kept her out of client meetings. Later on, during her first performance review, he wrote her up for her less-than-collegial behavior.

In a way, Lucy responded to her parents' unavailability by using her bluntness to try to convince others and herself that she didn't care. Deep down, she suffered from low self-esteem. Desperate for attention and approval, but distrusting that anyone would really care about her (as she felt her overwhelmed parents hadn't), she acted in ways that pushed people away when in fact she wanted to feel closer.

The real art of conversation is not only to say the right thing in the right place, but . . . to leave unsaid the wrong thing at the tempting moment.

—Dorothy Nevill

What's the difference, then, between being blunt and being direct? Think of tools. Blunt instruments are best for smashing rocks; they have no subtlety and don't take much intelligence to use. More specialized tools, like fine-edged circular saws, require skill and even artistry to use correctly. Carpenters get more respect than rock-smashers.

Lucy would have been more effective if she had tried to connect with people (which is what she wanted underneath) instead of being blunt and pushing them away. Everyone—she, her colleagues, her company, and her career—would have been the better for it.

Usable Insight

If you want to get your point across, be direct; if you want to destroy any chance of doing so, be blunt.

》》》 Action Steps

1. Next time you're tempted to spout off, count to three first. If what you have to say is more about getting attention or being critical rather than constructive, hold your fire.

2. Ask yourself what you are trying to accomplish by being blunt. If you want people to respect, like, and trust you, will being blunt have that effect?

3. If you say to yourself, "I don't care what people think of me," then ask yourself why you are trying so hard to get a reaction out of them.

4. Realize that though you may think other people's boundaries are dumb, those boundaries can be strictly enforced. Cross them at your peril.

5. Find a colleague at work who you see as being generally respected (this person should not be your boss or anyone in power). Notice how they listen to and reply to others. Pay attention to the language they use, including their body language, in meetings. Try emulating their style.

6. Next time you're tempted to react, think of a loving person in your life who has made you feel accepted—not for what you say but for who you are. Imagine their calm voice coaching you down from your high dive. Then ask yourself how this loving person would deal with the situation.

Chapter 22

Being Closed
Off to Input

Ardent clinging to one's opinion is the best
proof of stupidity.

—Michel de Montaigne

"JUST STOP IT! *That* doesn't help!" Rob snapped at me
with such ferocity that it made me jump. At six-foot-four,
Rob was imposing. As the senior "name" partner in a 120-
attorney law firm, he was hard-driving and imperious. As a
husband and father, he was unavailable and, on the occasions when he was present with his family, unpleasant.

A week after he'd been arrested for drunk driving, he
came to see me. Rob ran through his litany of complaints.
"Everybody in my life sucks—my ex-wife, my kids, my
practice, my staff—everybody."

"You must be feeling as overwhelmed and stressed out as you are ticked off," I responded with my best therapeutic-empathic tone.

"Stop being so goddamn understanding. You're like a frickin' vanilla milk shake! That is not what I need. All it does is make me angrier."

I found myself thinking of Billy Crystal's character in the movie *Analyze This*. Crystal plays a psychotherapist who gets sick of listening to the neurotic whining of his patients. In his imagination, he sees himself sternly and untherapeutically telling a weepy client to get over herself. I figured I had nothing to lose but this pain-in-the-rear patient, so I allowed life to imitate art.

I blurted out, "Rob! Just shut up and stop feeling so goddamn sorry for yourself."

We were both stunned. He stood up and came across the room. I prepared myself for a possible physical assault, but he stopped directly in front of me, broke into a big grin, said, "Exactly!" and proceeded to give me a big appreciative hug that lifted me off the floor.

Just as quickly, he sat down again, apparently much relieved. I half expected him to wag an approving index finger at me, just like Robert De Niro, and roll out a long "Yooooou."

"I don't get it," I told him. "You tell me how all the people in your life jump on your case and then you say that you want me to do the same thing. Maybe you just enjoy being jumped on."

"I want *you* to jump on me. You're a professional. I'm paying you to kick my ass. Everyone else . . ."

In truth, everyone in Rob's world was afraid of him. Rob's style at work was not unlike that of a Roman emperor. As chief rainmaker of his law firm, he dictated to everyone else. He didn't brook back talk. He heard what he wanted to hear. His firm was not growing as quickly as his competitors', with the result that the company was having trouble attracting high-quality candidates.

He tried to run his family the same way he ran his law firm, but they fought him. When they felt they weren't getting through to him, they raised the volume. The more they complained of his closed-off, dictatorial behavior, the more closed off and dictatorial he became. He was growing more and more isolated and bitter, and now he was taking risks with his life and the lives of others.

> Many are stubborn in pursuit of the path they have chosen, few in pursuit of the goal.
>
> —Friedrich Nietzsche

ROB WAS literally robbing himself of the chance to be helped by anyone. If it hadn't been for his DUI, he wouldn't even have come to me. But the DUI was a wake-up call. He knew his life was going awry, and he wanted to fix it before it was too late.

Therapy revealed that Rob was just acting the only way he knew. Raised by a critical, controlling, judgmental father and a mother who merely colluded in the father's dictatorship, Rob truly believed that being a man meant acting like his dad (see "Why We Get in Our Own Way" in the introduction). He also "heard" all input as critical, controlling, and judgmental, even if it wasn't.

During therapy, it also became clear to me why he had responded so well to my dressing-down. He was like a teenager who craved honest, direct input from a parent; in fact, his was a case of arrested development. (Teenagers are always looking for authoritative, nonauthoritarian figures to whom they can turn, despite all their rebellious bravado. When they can't find these authoritative figures, they feel angry and isolated and can act out in self-destructive ways.)

If any of this sounds familiar to you, it's probable that you, too, are primed to react to any input as if it is more authoritarian than authoritative. You may be stuck in a resentment from your teen years that you never moved beyond. Accordingly, you may be missing out on valuable input from people who, far from trying to control you as people may have done in the past, are truly trying to connect with you in your present life. If you continue to be a rebel without a cause by shutting off input, you will have to do everything on your own. You will miss out on great accomplishments, in both your work and your personal life.

USABLE INSIGHT

If you let the *authoritarian* figures from the past block input from *authoritative* figures in your life now, your future will die for the sins of your past.

▶▶▶ Action Steps

1. When someone close to you whom you believe to be on your side offers a suggestion, bite your lip and listen to it. Better yet, tell them you would like them to give you input whenever they see you doing something self-defeating, and then thank them for continuing to believe in you in spite of your behavior.

2. When someone at work offers you input, pause, listen, and say, "Thank you for the suggestion. You'll have to pardon my reaction, but when I get input and I'm not expecting it, it always catches me off guard." If you can do this, your graciousness will earn their respect.

3. Next time you shut off input from someone, rethink the situation. Recall people in your life, dead or alive, whom you truly respect. Ask yourself, "How would they handle this situation?"

4. If possible, seek those persons out and ask them directly for their input. Whenever you are faced with a situation that you would like to handle more effectively, remember their words. If these people are not available, use your imagination.

5. Counter the possible slide into self-righteousness by thinking of three things about you that make you difficult to deal with or, as they say, "a piece of work." Humility is the best antidote to many problems, including close-mindedness.

Chapter 23

Being
Unprepared

Spectacular achievement is always preceded
by unspectacular preparation.

—Robert H. Schu

MANY OF MY PATIENTS tell me of dreams in which
they find themselves back in school, having to take a test
for which they haven't studied sufficiently. In their waking
lives, most of these people tend to be prepared. The
dream is their fear, the opposite of who they are.

Then there are the people for whom everything is
impromptu. I remember one type A executive who was
under consideration for a big promotion. Bill had been
tapped to give a major presentation to the board of directors. For weeks he put off working on the presentation. It

seemed like the smallest of the fish he had to fry, and he was in a hurry to finish his other projects.

The night before the board meeting, Bill slapped a PowerPoint presentation together. He wasn't too worried. He was smart. He'd given many speeches before. He felt he knew his stuff cold.

The next day, in the middle of his talk, he realized he'd failed to include the details of some critical forecasting data. He skimmed over this fact, hoping no one would notice. But in the question-and-answer session, the chairman asked him about it. Bill was unable to answer and, embarrassed, promised the chairman that he'd "have to get back to you." His lack of preparedness had not spoken well of him. He was passed over for promotion, losing the job to a less experienced but clearly more prepared manager. That was his wake-up call.

To Bill's colleagues, the snubbing hadn't come as much of a surprise; they felt that he didn't deserve to be promoted anyway. He just seemed too arrogant. They secretly enjoyed his comeuppance.

Like so many who don't bother to prepare, Bill had two common problems discussed elsewhere in this book: He tended to procrastinate, and he lacked self-discipline. But another, deeper issue exacerbated these problems. He didn't prepare because he didn't think he had to.

Ever since he was a child, Bill had prepared only just enough to get by. As a student, instead of studying for a test over time, he'd stay up all night cramming. The fact that he managed to get reasonable grades without massive study convinced him that he was simply smarter than other people. He never got the stellar grades that might have landed him in an Ivy League school. Nevertheless, he graduated and found an entry-level job that allowed him to show off his smarts.

He developed a habit of "faking it till he made it," which carried him a long way in his professional life. Whenever he was under pressure, he assumed that his charisma, personality, ideas, and brilliance would win the day, as it always had. Used to running by the seat of his pants, he operated on an ingrained sense that all would be well, and if not, that all would at least be forgiven.

> Luck is a matter of preparation meeting opportunity.
> —Oprah Winfrey

IF YOU are someone who has been able to succeed or at least get by without preparing, you're not likely to change until you get that wake-up call. Maybe it will take getting fired or missing out on a great opportunity. But sooner or later, you realize that your persona, chutzpah, bravado, and bravura aren't enough. Even then, it may be too difficult to change something so deeply a part of you. Beating up on yourself or exercising sheer willpower may not be enough. Since ill-preparedness has probably cost you dearly already, it's time to swallow some pride.

One way to take a step in the right direction is to redo the presentation or project you messed up on because you were inadequately prepared—even if it's only for your own satisfaction. That's what Bill did. He redid his PowerPoint presentation, putting in all the information and slides he had omitted. When it was done, it was clear to him that had he offered this more thoughtful presentation, he would have won the promotion. To remind himself of his mistake, he made the missing slide from his presentation a screen saver on his computer.

While you're swallowing *your* pride, it's a good idea not to bite off more than you can chew, much less swallow. Start small and select a project for which you can properly prepare. It should be just enough so that you see the immediate payoff.

I like to think of the way Bruce Wright, a five-foot-eight competitive volleyball player, prepared as a high school player. He told me that he would lie on the floor of his bedroom with his head against the wall. From there, he would set a ball up until it "kissed" the ceiling (which was perfect set height) and do this five hundred times a day. After a while he never had to think of where a ball was coming from to set it up perfectly. The practice enabled him to focus on where everyone on the opposing team was playing. More important, it allowed him to focus on other things besides setting the ball, so that he could direct his team more effectively. Bruce can now boast that he's played competitively with the gold medal–winning U.S. Olympic team.

> One important key to success is self-confidence.
> An important key to self-confidence is preparation.
> —Arthur Ashe

Usable Insight

The respect you gain by being prepared is only exceeded by the respect you lose when you're not.

⟩⟩⟩ Action Steps

1. Think of the exact moment you lost that job, promotion, or opportunity due to lack of preparation. Remember it as clearly as possible. Don't berate yourself, but do conjure up intense emotions.

2. Ask yourself, "If I had this to do over, what could I have done differently that would have led to a positive result?" Even if you don't get a second chance, thinking about doing it over again will reinforce the lesson.

3. Set up a plan with a timeline, activities, and areas you would need to cover in order to better prepare yourself in the future. As painful as it is, think of a person who outperformed you—the person who received the plum job or project solely based on preparation. What did they do that you failed to do? (Alternatively, envision someone you know who prepares well and think of what they would do if they were in your position.)

4. If, after a period of two weeks, you have not been able to take action on this plan, don't berate yourself. Keep trying.

5. If all else fails, consider hiring a professional coach to keep you focused and on track and to hold you accountable for preparing for various activities in your job. If the best athletes need coaches to help them prepare, so might you.

Chapter 24

Being Afraid to Fire People

It isn't the people you fire who make your
life miserable, it's the people you don't.

—Harvey MacKay

ON THE POPULAR TELEVISION show *The Apprentice*, Donald Trump allows us all to give in to our voyeuristic impulses as we watch people try to scratch their way into a plum job working for one of the most arguably self-congratulatory bosses on earth. (It's amazing the lengths people will go to to flagellate themselves in public.) Self-promotion and bad hair aside, Trump does have one thing going for him (other than his fabulous wealth, of course): He knows how to let go of people who aren't working out well.

By contrast, plenty of managers have a terrible time telling bad employees to take a hike. Remember Deborah, the public relations manager in chapter 13 ("Feeling Guilty")? She tried to "repair" a recalcitrant employee who turned on her, and her own performance reviews suffered as a result. Instead of firing Joe, Deborah found herself on the firing line.

Certainly, on an objective level, it's often difficult to fire people. There are laws against wrongful termination, and most organizations only fire people whose behavior is extreme. Still, more than a few companies suffer when they hire the wrong person, especially for a key position. The time, money, and opportunity lost in discovering the mistake, terminating the individual, replacing him or her, undoing the damage, and then catching up to the competition is more than many companies can afford.

For her part, Deborah's fundamental problem was an inability to confront negative people (see "Fear of Confrontation"). As a manager, she should not have pandered to Joe. Instead she should have used performance reviews with tangible expectations and measurable results, as well as other HR processes, to winnow Joe out. By failing to do so, she allowed the dead wood to catch fire and burn her own house down.

> Give a lot, expect a lot, and if you don't get it, prune.
>
> —Tom Peters

THE MOST obvious way to avoid firing bad employees, of course, is to make sure that the right ones are on board in the first place. When Al Dorskind fired everyone at Universal Studios (see "Feeling Guilty") when they couldn't make the transition from a movie studio to a television studio, it gave management the opportunity to rehire the wheat and leave the chaff behind. Many of the poor performers made this easier by not reapplying because they secretly knew they were underperforming.

Of course, most managers don't have the power or the luxury to start with such a mass firing this way. But the best chance for objectivity occurs when you hire a new employee and when he or she leaves. It's important to filter out anyone who:

➤ **Does not take initiative.** His default mode is to be passive or reactive rather than proactive.

➤ **Won't make and keep commitments.** This person expects other people to do the work.

➤ **Doesn't and won't cooperate.** This person always finds some reason to say, "Yes, but . . ." and bails out on decisions made by others.

➤ **Refuses to be accountable for personal decisions, actions, and consequences.** He is unwilling to own up to mistakes and equally reluctant to pay the consequences. He thinks "I'm sorry" is sufficient.

➤ **Fails to learn from mistakes.** Everybody makes mistakes, but some people just keep making the same ones.

➤ **Has no imagination and is not curious.** This person would rather complain about what's wrong than come up with solutions that could make things better.

➤ **Lacks ethics.** You can't afford anyone who lacks the *judgment* to know the right thing to do, the *integrity* to do it, the *character* to stand up to those who don't, and the *courage* to stop those who won't.

USABLE INSIGHT

If you want to give your competition a great advantage, hold on to the people you should get rid of.

⟩⟩⟩ Action Steps

1. As a performance reviewer, you should make it your business to answer the following questions:
   - ✦ Would you rehire this person? If so, why? If not, why not?
   - ✦ If you were to rehire them, in what capacity could they best serve your company?
   - ✦ Knowing what you know about them now, what would you say their greatest strengths are? Their greatest weaknesses?
   - ✦ If you decide they're worth keeping, is there a way to help them maximize their strengths? (Marcus Buckingham's landmark book *Now, Discover Your Strengths* can help you understand better how to do this.)

2. **Use "The Self-Other Inventory" (Appendix 4)**
   This tool helps you to evaluate people for a performance review; it also lessens the stress of doing one by helping to make explicit, realistic expectations for your people. (Don't confuse reasonable with realistic expectations. Reasonable makes sense; realistic is what is likely to happen. For example, it's reasonable to expect an employee to learn a new software tool; it's unrealistic to expect technically challenged people to master it.) You can use the tool to discuss your observations and ask the employee how he or she might see things differently. It also logically leads to areas of needed improvement.

   To create your own Self-Other Inventory, refer to the chart in appendix 4.

Chapter 25

Expecting Your Boss to Appreciate You

The wheel that squeaks the loudest is the one that gets the grease.

—Josh Billings

FROM THE START, Charlene had been a star. She was recruited by the company from a competitor, and her boss was thrilled to have her on board. Expectations were high.

Within two years, she had met them. Month after month, Charlene pulled solid sales numbers. She logged innumerable frequent-flier miles to meet with prospects and clients. She came up with creative new strategies. She was one of the best performers on her team. Or so she thought.

So when her boss, Jim, announced that he was going to schedule "check-in" lunches with each of the team members to discuss their progress, she fully expected him to discuss her inevitable raise and probable promotion.

But after salad, salmon, crème brûlée, and coffee, the word "raise" never raised its head. Instead, her boss asked her about projects she was working on, and asked her to discuss client issues. When the discussion finally came around to her performance, all he said was "keep up the good work."

Finally Charlene decided to broach the subject herself: "Jim, I think I'm due for a raise."

Jim took a large swallow of coffee. "That's interesting." He raised an inquisitorial eyebrow. "Why?"

Charlene pointed out everything from her "have done" list, and threw in a few additional pieces of ammunition, including two unassigned projects. Then she pointed out that she had done more work than her colleagues, and listed the number of accounts she'd pursued.

"That's great, Charlene," Jim said, "but I'm not sure a raise is in order right now. The rest of the team has been working pretty hard, too. How about a little extra time off as a reward for now? I'm sure you're tired and could use it."

Charlene reddened. It was as if she had been riding an elevator to the top floor and suddenly the cable snapped. She had gone from feeling on top of the world to crashing. She felt angry but tried not to show it.

That night, she complained to her husband that her boss didn't appreciate her. She talked seriously about quitting. After taking a few days off, she returned, feeling bruised, and began polishing up her résumé.

Ironically, her boss *had* thought about giving her a raise at year's end, though he wasn't prepared to discuss it at the time. But he was taken aback by her brazen and sudden appeal—and particularly by the comparison to her teammates.

Okay, so you go into situations expecting or feeling a certain sense of entitlement. It's human nature to think more about what *you* want and need than what others want and need from you—after all, we can't read minds. Chances are you have never been very conscious about evaluating the companies you work for. You're accomplished enough; you think your résumé and education speak for themselves. You think you're a wunderkind. You think your boss is already so impressed with you that he won't bother looking closer.

It is also common not to think of the big goals of your company or your boss. You assume that since he or she went to the trouble of hiring you that they are happy to have you around. As long as you do your work, contribute to the bottom line, and don't make waves, you're good. You also tend to believe that working hard gives you extra credit.

But, my friend, working hard is not the same as working smart.

Before asking for a raise, Charlene might have thought about Jim's point of view. He managed not only her, but other people as well—including the "people upstairs." His boss expected a lot from him. He was under terrific time pressure. He was under intense pressure to contribute more to the bottom line. He probably didn't get enough sleep. The last thing he needed to deal with was a demand from a staffer whom he'd just invited to a friendly lunch. If Charlene really wanted to get on the right side of her boss, she might have stopped thinking about what she deserved and started thinking about what it would take to make his life easier.

Here's the bottom line: Your boss probably doesn't care about who you are or what you know. He wants to know what you've done for him. Do something that makes your boss look good to his or her boss or that helps his career, and you'll be more likely to receive the reward you want. Find out what your boss wants and needs most, then do it in such a way that it gets noticed (without your having to call attention to it). Achieve great results with a minimum of training or hand-holding, and your boss will quickly recognize the value of your work.

> You can get everything in life you want if you will just help enough other people get what they want.
>
> —Zig Ziglar

WHAT EXACTLY does your boss want from you?

➤ *More.* Whether people own up to it or not, everybody wants more. Getting more from you than he expects gives your boss the feeling that he's smart for having you on his team.

➤ *Better.* Even bosses who desire quantity seek out quality in your work product. Being able to help produce high-quality results that exceed the expectations of not only your boss but his boss as well, will do wonders for your perceived worth.

➤ *Faster.* Time is money. Your boss may bark at you to speed things up because his superiors are breathing down his neck to do the same. If you can deliver results sooner than your boss expects, without diminishing the quality or making mistakes, it distinguishes you from the other employees who have trouble meeting deadlines.

➤ *Cheaper.* Your boss has to make do with a budget. If your results far exceed the cost of your project—or better yet, the cost of your employment—you're a star. Even considering the cost factor in what you do sets you apart from others.

➤ *Safer.* As much as some bosses like the excitement of a pedalto-the-metal, throw-caution-to-the-wind project, the potential slips and slides scare them more. Be someone who helps your boss safely take on bigger and better projects.

An effort in any one of these areas will help you stand out and collect the raise you deserve.

USABLE INSIGHT

Do unto your boss before you expect him or her to do unto you.

▶▶▶ Action Steps

1. When thinking of asking for a raise or a promotion, ask and answer the question: "Why do you think you deserve it? And why now?"
2. Pick a time when you've achieved a big win for your boss.
3. Try to be considerate. If you must ask for something, never ask for anything inappropriate or at an inappropriate time. If you must ask for something, pick a time when your boss is in a generous mood.
4. If you want to propose something new, think it through first and address any objections. How would you respond to them?
5. During your next performance review, ask your boss what goals you will need to meet going forward to qualify you for your next raise or promotion.
6. Finally, mentally prepare yourself for meetings with your boss with this piece of wisdom in mind: "Have high hopes and realistic expectations, but don't count on anything."

Chapter 26

Fear of Giving or Receiving Performance Reviews

> Negative feedback is better than none. I would rather have a man hate me than overlook me. As long as he hates me I make a difference.
>
> —Hugh Prather

WHAT A *LOVELY* SENTIMENT about feedback! Is this a case where Hugh Prather "doth protest too much"? Perhaps he *is* being completely sincere, but the level of your cynicism or at least skepticism regarding his quote will reveal to you the discomfort—if not paranoia—with which you approach the subject of feedback, whether you are receiving or giving it.

Performance reviews are one of the ugliest facts of life in any company. Most bosses I know hate giving them because they feel like they have to walk on eggshells when delivering criticism. And for most employees, performance reviews are like an unpleasant medical test or examination (think "pelvic" or "prostate") involving the psychological equivalent of prodding, cold poking, and unforgiving plastic. It's an annual or semiannual ritual that must be faced, however ugly it may be.

> "Constructive criticism" is a scam run by people who want to beat you up. And they want you to believe they are doing it for your own good.
>
> —Cheri Huber

SOME PEOPLE on the receiving end panic in the face of performance reviews, particularly if they know they have not done as well as they expected to do, for whatever reasons (these may be real or imagined).

One woman I know, Vicky, had been through a rough year at home. She had lived through an illness in her family that had caused her to miss a few important deadlines and take extended time off. She loved her job and prided herself on her work. But she was certain that her "slacking" would be an object of serious discussion on the Day of Atonement. She grew so nervous about the meeting with her boss that she called in sick the day it was to take place. She had made herself physically sick with worry.

> People ask for criticism, but they only want praise.
>
> —W. Somerset Maugham

FEEDBACK BY itself is a neutral term. It is likely to be as positive as it is negative. So why is it that you are so resistant receiving your performance review? As is the case with many such fears, this one arises from fear of criticism instilled early in childhood. Highly critical parents do a kind of Vulcan mind control on their children, to the point that even loving correction sounds to a child like harsh criticism. Criticism is such a loud, overriding message that it obliterates all others.

And children of critical parents tend to have brittle self-images. If you were criticized as a child, chances are you may work incredibly hard to prove yourself, and you do. But you aren't a very happy camper, particularly when evaluation time rolls around.

Ironically, part of what perpetuates the lack of efficacy in most feedback is the awkwardness of many bosses in giving it. If you manage other people, you may well project onto them how upset, hurt, or angry you were in the past in receiving feedback. It's as if you are taking painstaking steps to avoid provoking in your employees what was provoked in you when you received feedback.

But in an effort not to hurt an employee's feelings or provoke anger, you can come off as so tentative that it adds insult to injury. You and your employee know that his or her performance may not have been perfect during the year. But your awkwardness seems to prolong the agony of your employee finding out what the "punishment" is (in terms of "areas of improvement" or "next year's goals"). Like an adolescent, your employee would probably prefer a quick spanking to a drawn-out lecture.

How can both of you escape this vicious cycle? Since the purpose of feedback is not to hurt, punish, or humiliate, but rather to provide employees with the chance to be more effective in the future, the goal on both parts should be to neutralize the fear you both feel.

The chance to do something right in the future is much more motivating than having to do penance for doing something wrong in the past.

Action Steps for Feedback-Receivers

If you are on the receiving end of the performance review, then you can circumvent your own and your boss's fears by being proactive in assessing yourself, developing realistic goals, creating a solid support system, and rewarding yourself for your achievements when you do overcome an obstacle.

Executive coach Marshall Goldsmith has developed the concept of "feed-forward" to help people deal with "no win" situations. Here's how it works:

1. Select superiors, peers, or subordinates who have a stake in your being more effective (that is, who would benefit from your improved performance).

2. Tell them that you are working on professional development and want to improve your effectiveness in working with each of them.

3. With step 2 in mind, ask each of your "stakeholders" to tell you what observable and distinct behaviors you could improve upon going forward that would increase their respect, ease, and effectiveness in working with you. (It's what I call "assertive humility," and it is very disarming.)

4. Try to listen without becoming defensive. Be as objective as possible. Ask them to elaborate on things that are unclear to

you, so you both know exactly the behavior they would like you to change.

5.   After you understand and articulate to them what you understand the desired change(s) to be, reiterate: "So, if I were to change and sustain changes in X and Y behavior going forward, you would be able to let go of the past problems we've had and give our working together another chance. Is that what you mean?"

You can tell how this approach can create tremendous "buy-in" (see "Not Getting Buy-In") and then, one hopes, cooperation and a new lease on the way you work together.

▶▶▶ Action Steps for Feedback-Givers

1.   Refer to "The Self-Other Inventory" in chapter 24 and appendix 4.

2.   Instead of waiting to give corrective feedback in one unpleasant session, nip problems in the bud—or even before they are buds. It's much more difficult to correct a problem once it has gained momentum.

3.   Ask employees to do a self-assessment before the formal review takes place. That way, your employee will come prepared with his or her own self-criticism, which takes the onus off you. Then you can discuss issues more openly (and comfort people who may have been too hard on themselves, as many are likely to be).

4.   During the review, dissipate your fear-based awkwardness by talking openly about the discomfort you have felt in receiving

and giving feedback, then move directly into a positive discussion about what the employee has done well during the year.

5. Focus on the future. Don't spend a lot of time talking about past performance. Rather, make the discussion about future goals and effective performance. Specific goals—preferably with timelines and deliverables—can give the employee something to work on immediately.

Chapter 27

Confusing Dumping with Venting

They may forget what you said, but they will
never forget how you made them feel.
—Carl W. Buechner

MEGAN LISTENED CAREFULLY as her colleague
Jennifer vented over lunch about another coworker. "You
know, Diane is not as smart as the boss thinks she is,"
Jennifer said. "It just makes me crazy to see the way he
caters to her. She has completely pulled the wool over
his eyes."

Megan agreed, then grasped the opportunity to do a
little venting herself. "Well, you know, he is hardly the most
objective person in the world," she said. "I mean, he sees
what he wants to see." She felt her cheeks go a little hot as

she remembered the way the boss had flippantly—or so it seemed to Megan—dismissed a proposal that she believed was very good.

Suddenly, Megan began pouring out her resentment against the boss. Not only did he play favorites, but he was close-minded and narcissistic. He reminded Megan of her ex-husband, who thought he was God's gift to women but who, in fact, turned out to be a coward and a philanderer. This was turning into a long "dumping" session about her ex-husband, then men in general.

Jennifer sat silently while Megan rolled into an increasingly out-of-control diatribe. "Wow," Jennifer thought, "Megan really has a problem." After that, she stopped asking Megan to lunch, thinking that anyone who was that hostile was someone to be avoided.

Jennifer began the conversation by venting a bit about Diane; Megan returned the venting with dumping.

What's the difference?

We all need to vent our frustration at times. If we do it with people we trust and who trust us in return, it's helpful and useful in maintaining our composure. Jennifer needed to let off a little steam regarding Diane with a colleague with whom she had *presumed* such trust existed. Megan tested that friendship by taking her complaints too far—dumping on her boss, then her ex-husband, then men in general.

Dumping is literally a verbal avalanche that buries others. It's a scary thing, to be buried under someone's mental and verbal snow; you feel suffocated and then resentful.

What causes you to dump? First, you probably lack an effective way to address the person who is really upsetting you (see "Fear of Confrontation"), so you feel you need to periodically let off steam on someone else to keep yourself from exploding altogether. All too often, however, when you hold in upset feelings and are finally given the opportunity to vent, you find yourself wanting to take the chance to let it all out until you are spent.

Kids in junior high school, and often in high school, get into the habit of dumping because misery loves company. Dumping is a way for adolescents to feel better in two ways. First, verbally expressing frustration, disappointment, and upset displaces the impulse they have to act out physically (such as through violence, drug use, or other destructive behaviors including eating disorders). Second, dumping on peers helps adolescents feel less alone and self-righteously justified. It's as if they've created a herd to follow their cause.

As an adult, dumping has the opposite of the herding effect. It can create a tremendous disconnect between you and the person who's suffering under the avalanche, because with every passing moment that you feel relieved, they begin to feel more frustrated and put-upon.

> You can build a throne with bayonets, but you can't sit on
> it for long.
>
> —Boris Yeltsin

WHEN YOU dump rather than vent, the person to whom you are speaking will feel as if you are running over them (see "Talking Over or At Others") and turn off. Worse, they feel "dumped on."

When you feel you need to vent, the challenge is to keep it from turning into dumping. That is, you want to prevent venting from crossing over into something that comes back to bite you. (For instance, Jennifer could easily have spread the word about Megan's attitude, which might ultimately have reached the boss, but she chose to simply avoid Megan.) To do this, you need to find healthier ways to deal with your feelings about the person who is frustrating you (see "Fear of Confrontation" for help with this).

Additionally, when you learn to forgive (see "Not Forgiving") and discover ways to overcome your frustration (see "Becoming Frustrated"), you can get at the root of the dumping and break the habit.

Usable Insight

Don't confuse verbal relief with real resolution.

>>> Action Steps

1. Realize that when you go on and on (endlessly or on different occasions) about something that's bothering you, you're not venting, you're dumping—and turning sympathizers and people who root for you into ones who root against you. Your rant may make you feel better, but it makes others feel worse.

2. Check yourself. Remember the conversation. If you dumped, apologize to the other person for having done so. Ask them to help you decipher whether you were really just venting or truly dumping.

3. Realize that venting may bring you relief, but it doesn't resolve anything. Develop a more effective approach to the people or situations that frustrate you by reviewing the chapters on "Fear of Confrontation" and "Becoming Frustrated."

Chapter 28

Fear of Confrontation

Tolerance is a very dull virtue. It is boring.
Unlike love, it has always had a bad press. It
is negative. It merely means putting up with
people, being able to stand things.

— E. M. Forster

FRANK WAS, by all measures, a Silicon Valley success. The overachieving, Stanford-educated, thirty-nine-year-old founder and CEO of a fifty-person software company, Frank lived in a large, well-appointed house in tony Palo Alto, California. He had plenty of money in the bank, backed by plenty of promise from the venture capital community.

Despite his outward success, Frank found his work life

was a paradox. He'd achieved his dream of starting and running his own company, but he loathed his job. In fact, he so dreaded going to work every day that he would sometimes just duck out to the golf course, leaving everyone wondering where he was and who would make the decisions. One day, Frank missed a critical meeting, and the company lost an important contract.

Suspecting a problem—a woman? drugs?—the board called him on the carpet, and called me in to run interference. The appointment was made.

It's a terrible thing to see a tall, good-looking, well-educated, accomplished, driven, and otherwise intelligent man—the good kid—caught playing truant. "I'm no slacker," he said at the outset, and I believed him. The story was that Frank just "couldn't stand" the board-appointed CFO—a grouchy man fifteen years Frank's senior who, according to Frank's description, made Scrooge sound fairly generous. Even the sound of Mike's gruff voice stressed Frank out. The week before, after overhearing Mike browbeating a vendor on the phone, Frank's neck went out.

"Some days I get so frustrated with Mike that I take off for an extended lunch, or just leave early," Frank told me.

"But what about the other employees who are stuck working with this guy?" I asked.

"Well, since I'm the founder, I felt I could make my own schedule." He paused. "Everyone else just has to put up with him, I guess. We need him. But . . . we all feel better when Mike's out sick."

"So when he's not out sick, *you* call in sick."

Silence.

"Do you think Mike was the reason you lost that woman in your accounting department?"

"HR did a closing interview, but they didn't say her boss was the reason," he answered. "But yes, now that you mention it, I'm sure that's why she left. Mike was a real son of a bitch to her. To everyone. Nobody likes him."

"Maybe HR didn't tell you because they knew you wouldn't do anything about it," I ventured. "Maybe the employee left not just because she resented Mike, but because she was more disappointed in you."

Frank didn't run his company; Mike did. Everyone at the firm seemed to realize that Frank was in denial, terrified of confronting the reality of The Ogre. How could the boss be so blind?

Like anyone in thrall to negative people, Frank had no idea that catastrophe was imminent. He had allowed Mike's influence to corrode his life, far beyond merely stunting his job enthusiasm. Employees resented Frank's passivity. The board suspected him of incompetence. Investors raised eyebrows. His kids wondered where Daddy was. His wife contemplated divorce. His dream job was on the line. In his psychologically cocooned mode, Frank had not the foggiest idea.

Why don't we stand up to people who, day after day, sap our enthusiasm and vitality, and poison the lives of everyone around us? Is it that we're afraid we'll provoke them into losing control and doing something to hurt us? Or is it that we don't want to provoke them?

Most psychologists will tell you right off that your failure to confront negative people springs from your familial coping strategy. Frank, for example, was the child of a gruff, alcoholic father who verbally and physically abused his children. Confrontation—which he witnessed when his mother fought back—only brought on more abuse. So, like any smart and reasonable kid, Frank skipped town. He spent as little time at home as possible when his father was around, though he secretly yearned for his father's approval. He compensated by earning approval in the great, abstract, patriarchal institution of school. But multiple degrees did not confer freedom. As an overachieving adult, he still remained transfixed by this beloved but berating figure, whose familiar role had been transferred to the respected-but-fearsome Mike.

In the next session with Frank, I learned that an even deeper fear controlled him. It is a fear that seems counterintuitive when you're ducking confrontation. It turned out that Frank was frightened to the very bone that *he* would lose control with Mike. Like most of us, Frank liked to think of himself as intelligent, reasonable, and calm. Confronting this grouchy, touchy pseudo-father—against whom he'd built such a store of anger—might throw him off balance. What if Mike's reaction were extreme—as Frank expected it would be, given what he had witnessed in his own father? If this happened, Frank's psychological gunpowder might ignite. He might lose control. He might go ballistic. He might even . . .

And so he chose to remain calm, collected—and irresponsible.

The Australian medical pioneer Sister Elizabeth Kenny noted that "he who angers you, conquers you." Now the question is: How can you confront negative people without blowing up at them? How do you tell them off without losing control and risking escalation or retaliation?

> One man with courage makes a majority.
> —Andrew Jackson

YOU NEED a *replacement coping strategy*. Specifically, a replacement coping strategy changes the power dynamic and turns four significant psychological tables at once. By finding a principle to stand up for, instead of focusing your aggression on your opponent, you stay centered, become empowered, and shoot from your head instead of your hip. You follow the dictum:

$$\text{Aggression} + \text{Principle} = \text{Conviction}$$
$$\text{Aggression} - \text{Principle} = \text{Hostility}$$

What happens when you apply this strategy to a person who is doing the wrong thing? First, it sets forth the expected rules of behavior by basing your aggressive reaction to the negative person on principle as opposed to deteriorating into a finger-pointing, zero-sum game. Working from principle eases the depressing weight of having to take responsibility for the other person's junk. It ropes their responsibility to a general "law" or principle ("You ran the stop light").

Likewise, instead of triggering resentment and defensiveness in other people, standing on principle makes *them* seek *your* approval. It also puts the negative person on his or her guard by sending the message that you are the traffic cop. If they do not play by the rules, they will have to face the consequences. Thus you reclaim your power and authority.

Finally, operating from principle allows you to see your antagonists in another light. By opening the door—even just a little—to what they bring to the table, you create the surprising possibility for change.

Frank found that standing up for a principle I call "root for you or root against you" was amazingly simple and effective. The key to this principle is to look for something—anything—you can possibly (and honestly) value in the negative person. Is there something in their intelligence, forthrightness, cleverness, assertiveness, honesty, or anything else that you, however begrudgingly, admire? Use what you honestly value in that person as a lever. This means telling the negative person that you want to "root for" them on the basis of their talents and contributions, but you're having difficulty doing that. The goal is to get your opponent to change their behavior or leave.

Armed with the principle of "root for you or root against you," Frank thought about the things Mike brought to the table. Mike knew what he was doing. He had extensive experience with successful companies. He had an awesome track record. He had taken several private firms public. He had good relationships with venture capitalists, and so on. The next morning Frank called Mike into his office and told him, in all sincerity, that he wanted to root for him, and listed all the reasons why. "Mike," he said, "you are a gifted CFO. You are wonderfully experienced. The board believes in you. You are important to this company."

Then he delivered the bad news. He was having difficulty rooting for him because Mike's negative behavior had made it truly hard for others to work there. "Mike," Frank said resolutely, "I feel dangerously close to rooting against you. You intimidate people and get *good* results, when you could be inspiring them and getting *great* results. People are afraid of you, not because you're too demanding but because you're demeaning. I know this doesn't make sense, because your way has worked for you during your long, successful career. But nobody is going to be afraid to come to work at this company from now on. Nobody! Either you need to change *how* you work, or you need to change *where* you work."

Frank's tone revealed his own real regret at the prospect of such a talented person leaving the company, but it rested squarely on his resolve that his company had to be a safe place to work.

And here's the shocker: Mike was *thankful for the honest feedback*. He even admitted he had a problem. "Most people just choose not to deal with me," Mike confessed. His attitude and behavior had run him into problems with people elsewhere, but no one was forthright enough to tell him directly. In the end, Mike became a better colleague, Frank stayed in his job, and the company grew by leaps and bounds.

▶▶▶ Action Steps

1. Take out a sheet of paper and draw a vertical line down the center.
2. On the left side, write down the names of all the negative people that suck the life out of you and whom you dread seeing.
3. On the right side, write the names of all the people who give you energy and motivate you.
4. Find a principle to stand up for.
5. Confront the negative people by showing your regret that you are beginning to root against them.
6. Make a thirty-day commitment to minimize the time you spend with the energy drainers and maximize your time with the energy suppliers (and then continue this strategy for life).

Chapter 29

Making Excuses

> It is wise to direct your anger towards
> problems—not people; to focus your energies
> on answers—not excuses.
>
> —William Arthur Ward

"I HAD NO OTHER CHOICE but to rush the order through to get it out on time," Paul explained. Paul worked at a high-end computer peripheral company and had just been called on the carpet for a customer receiving a damaged unit.

"It shouldn't have been a surprise that there would be some errors," he went on breathlessly. "You can't rush things and have them turn out perfectly. There was no time to check with the mail room to make certain the packing was secure. I did all I could, given the time pressure we were under. It was just bad luck that the part arrived damaged and unusable when it got to the customer. It's totally unfair that I had to pay for the damaged part! I think I had every right to make an issue out of it."

In the course of a few minutes, Paul had offered five different explanations for his error: having no choice, being rushed, not checking with the mail room, unfairness at the top, and bad luck.

Just about everyone believes that an explanation is sufficient to get them off the hook, regardless of the power they wield or the responsibility they have. Enron's Ken Lay *explained* that he knew nothing about what his senior managers were doing in cooking the books. Walt Disney CEO Michael Eisner *explained* his decision to pay his ex–best friend, Michael Ovitz, an exorbitant severance package.

Everyone has an explanation. But an explanation is, purely and simply, an excuse—despite the fact that some people try to ennoble themselves by saying, "This is an explanation, not an excuse." And it's funny how people who can't stand to hear an explanation or an excuse from someone else think that their own explanations and excuses should be taken as legitimate.

> He that is good for making excuses is seldom good for anything else.
>
> —Benjamin Franklin

WHY DO you continue to think that explanations excuse you even when your explanations are obviously lame? When will you understand that when you make a mistake that affects others, they really don't want to know why you made it?

Even if your boss says to you, "How could you do that?" it's important to understand that he is not asking for an explanation or even an answer. "How could you do that?" is actually a statement in a question's clothing. What your boss is really saying is: "I can't believe you did that. Now what the heck are we going to do?" But he won't say that out loud. Why? Because it's easier to blame you than own up to the fact that something you did now makes him vulnerable. He looks bad because of your mistake; he feels he has to clean it up.

How do you fall into the excuse-making habit to begin with? You probably received your training in your family:

"Mommy, Johnny hit me with a rock!"
"Johnny, why did you hit your sister?"
"I didn't throw it at her. She was standing in the way!"

When you grow up with people who blame you, you automatically assume a defensive posture when you mess up. Your explanations are not just a way to avoid punishment. Ironically and poignantly, they are a sad effort to regain dignity when you're embarrassed. You want more than anything else to be forgiven and feel exonerated. When you explain your bad behavior, you're trying to evoke a soothing "It's all right" response that you may still be looking for from a parent.

The worst thing about explanations is that even when they make you feel like you're off the hook, they just make things worse. Explanations make you look more foolish than ever.

Taking responsibility for your mistakes, by contrast, gets you out of your childish mode; it recovers your dignity. Mature people understand that mistakes happen in the workplace. Responsibility is not about guilt and punishment. Rather it is a case of recognizing and correcting your mistakes as soon as possible so you can get back on track with whatever you are trying to accomplish (see "Not Learning from Your Mistakes").

One of the most important tasks of a manager is to eliminate his people's excuses for failure.

—Robert Townsend

THE TRICK for avoiding explanations and excuses is to separate your goals at work from your feelings of defensiveness. If the goal is to learn and grow, you have to own up to your mistakes and correct them. No amount of talk will change anything. If Paul had understood this, he might have taken a different stance and said something like this to his boss:

"I made a mistake in shipping a faulty part to the customer. I tried to rush things and quality suffered as a result. I will do everything I can to correct my work in the future. I appreciate your input, and ask you to tell me what I can do to make amends so that we can move forward."

USABLE INSIGHT

Explanations don't excuse—and excuses don't excuse either.

▶▶▶ Action Steps

1. Recognize when you have made a mistake as soon as you can. One way to monitor your behavior is to imagine anything you say or do on the front page of your city's newspaper. If you would be hesitant to have it be where everyone can see, you've probably made a mistake that you don't want people to know about.

2. When you make a mistake, take responsibility immediately. Don't offer explanations unless they are asked for, and then

only in the service of your honest apology. Here are potential scripts:

"I tried A and:

- it did work and then I did . . .
- it didn't work and then I did . . .
- discovered I didn't know how to do it and then I did . . .
- discovered I did it wrong and then I did . . .

3. Create a plan for doing damage control, correcting the mistake so it doesn't recur and making amends to any injured parties so that everyone can get back on track as soon as possible.

4. Realize that the workplace is not your family. Mistakes are not about punishment, retaliation, or humiliation. They are an opportunity to learn.

Chapter 30

Focusing on
Your Weaknesses

> I worshipped dead men for their strength,
> forgetting I was strong.
>
> —Vita Sackville-West

"SINCE WHEN IS FOCUSING on your weaknesses a self-defeating behavior?" you ask. "After all, isn't this entire book about identifying self-defeating behaviors—which are weaknesses—and overcoming them?"

Now I've thoroughly confused you, but read on.

In his landmark book *Now, Discover Your Strengths*, Gallup Poll researcher Marcus Buckingham posited that people actually perform much better when they play to their strengths rather than attempt to fix their weaknesses.

Now, I want to make a distinction between a weakness and a self-defeating behavior. In workplace parlance, a weakness—as your boss has undoubtedly pointed out in past performance reviews (see "Fear of Giving or Receiving Performance Reviews")—generally refers to a skill that needs improvement. Unfortunately, most performance reviews focus on weaknesses rather than on strengths. And even more unfortunately, most of us tend to remember criticism rather than praise. Your boss may not only say that you had a good year but also that you can do better if you sell more, shore up your computer or writing skills, or work a bit harder at managing your time.

A self-defeating behavior, on the other hand, is more than a weakness; it is a psychological block that keeps you from performing well in the first place. The problem is that focusing on weakness causes you to lose self-confidence—and this begins to evoke some of the self-defeating behaviors described in this book.

For instance, if your boss tells you positive things, but also that you need to learn to delegate better or that you procrastinate, you may lose perspective. You start berating yourself, telling yourself to delegate better or stop procrastinating, rather than putting effort into the areas that you like and in which you excel—the areas of your strengths and your keys to success. But when you beat up on yourself about your productivity, you can become even less productive.

According to Buckingham, it's often a waste of time to try to strengthen your weaknesses—that is, the skills you lack—when research shows that in general your weaknesses don't really get better; in fact, for many people, they tend to get worse over time. On the other hand, finding and focusing on your strengths is a winning formula.

Consider one of Buckingham's best examples, famed UCLA coach John Wooden. Wooden said that the secret to his success (as the best college basketball coach ever) was his ability to assemble a team of great players, then discover and develop each individual's strength.

Then he would compel the team to play from its group strength. If he had a team of particularly good shooters one year, he'd run a shooting game; if another year he had great passers, he'd run a passing game, and so on. Wooden knew that trying to turn his shooters into passers, and his passers into shooters, was a waste of time; it was better to encourage the natural skills of the individuals on the team.

> Don't let what you cannot do interfere with what you can.
>
> —John Wooden

IF YOU manage other people, think about applying Wooden's lessons. But if you are in turn managed, you needn't wait for your boss to identify your strengths for you. To identify your true strengths—that is, to discover what natural talents and abilities you have—take a survey of people around you and ask them what *they* think you are good at. Once you have a consensus, focus on developing those strengths so that you can be all that you can be; then find people who are good at the things you aren't to partner with you.

You will discover that when you play to your strengths not only will you accomplish more, but it becomes much easier to deal with challenges and setbacks. For if you fall down doing something you're good at and about which you're usually passionate, you can more easily pick yourself up and try again.

USABLE INSIGHT

Over time, your weaknesses generally become worse. And if you focus too much on them, so, too, will your strengths.

▶▶▶ Action Steps

Fill in the blanks:

1. The areas of my job I am most competent in and passionate about are _____. (Ask your friends, coworkers, and bosses for their input.)

2. The areas in which I have the least competence and passion are _____. The best people to do those functions are _____ because they _____.

3. If I developed _____ or could accomplish _____ in my particular area(s) of competence and passion, it would greatly increase my effectiveness on the job.

4. If I achieved _____, it would give me the leverage to delegate my tasks of lowest competence and passion to _____ so that I could continue to focus on my greatest strengths.

Chapter 31

Being Impulsive

A conclusion is the place where you got
tired of thinking.

—Steven Wright

MANNY WAS A SMART, talented, creative account
manager for a large advertising agency. He loved his work;
his colleagues and clients loved him. He was funny and
outgoing.

He also had a tendency to act before thinking, which
on more than one occasion had landed him in water that,
while not quite boiling, was distinctly warm.

Manny's boss had confided to him that another account
manager, Jason, seemed to be having trouble coming up to
speed. After this confidence, Manny took it upon himself

to be a hero to both his boss and Jason. He invited Jason for a drink after work, thinking he might be able to help his colleague learn the ropes more quickly. Over a few beers, he asked Jason all kinds of questions, and dug to find out what difficulties he might be encountering. When they parted ways, Manny felt happy.

The next day, Manny's boss confronted him, asking what exactly he had told Jason.

Manny felt embarrassed and tried to remember what he might have said that would be upsetting his boss. He was tongue-tied. So his boss pursued it:

"Did you say anything about his progress here?"

Manny explained that he thought he was doing the right thing by taking Jason out for a friendly drink and offering some coaching tips.

His boss countered that she wished Manny hadn't acted so impulsively. She had spoken with Jason earlier that morning and was surprised to learn that Manny had made some suggestions that she found questionable. "I wish you would think before you act, Manny," she said finally. "Or at least check in with me before you decide you're going to be someone else's coach."

> Everything comes gradually and at its appointed hour.
>
> —Ovid

ALL HIS LIFE, Manny had been impulsive, but the reasons weren't biological. He didn't have the kind of impulsivity that people associate with attention deficit disorder. Rather, Manny had a bad habit of speaking and acting before he had thought matters through or considered the consequences. It was as if he felt he had to shoot on reflex, like a trigger-happy hunter.

If you are impulsive, it may be that you are in love with your ideas. In fact, you're so infatuated with them that you drown out thoughts of the consequences of your actions. Manny, for example, wasn't trying to hurt anyone. His motives were fine. He just failed to think about what might happen when he "investigated" Jason.

Impulsiveness like Manny's is fundamentally a benign form of impatience. It's not the ugly, stormy impatience that feels like overwhelming anger; rather, it's a desire to react. In both cases, impatience drives you to make uninformed snap judgments and react in ways you'll later regret.

Alternatively, impulsiveness can be caused by the feeling that unless you say or do something *now*, you will forget to do it later. In your mind you think, "Better now than never," for the buildup of tension and angst from holding back feels unbearable to you. In both these instances, your mind has a mind of its own—and it's not working in your best interest.

Somewhere during your life you chose impulsivity rather than the alternative of keeping a lid on it. You may have grown up in a family that lacked boundaries and found yourself surrounded by a sea of similarly impulsive people. You may have felt pressured to fit in.

How do you overcome impulsiveness? The most important thing to do is to be aware of your triggers. To do this, you need to step outside yourself and identify the times when you feel like reacting. By not giving in to the urge to respond immediately to statements and situations, you may find that you are able to achieve much more and improve your image and reputation as a team player or a manager. More important, you will be seen as someone who can be trusted and respected.

Have patience with all things, but chiefly have patience with yourself.

—Saint Francis de Sales

▶▶▶ Action Steps

Take your finger off the trigger by increasing and shifting your awareness. This will lessen the intensity of the impulse.

The following Six-Step Pause exercise will help:

Step 1: Become physically aware.
A physical sensation is usually one of the earliest signals that you're in reactive mode. Identify what you're feeling—prickliness, tightness in your stomach or neck, light-headedness, and so on.

Step 2: Become emotionally aware.
Attach an emotion to the physical sensation, as in: "I feel excited, frustrated, afraid, hurt," and so on.

Fill in the blanks for the following steps:

Step 3: Become aware of the impulse.
"Feeling [the emotion in step 2] makes me want to_____."

Step 4: Become aware of consequences.
"The likely result if I act on that impulse is _____."

Step 5: Become aware of solutions.
"A better thing to do would be _____."

Step 6: Become aware of benefits.
"If I follow the solution in step 5, the benefit is likely to be _____."

Chapter 32

Becoming Frustrated

Our fatigue is often caused not by work, but
by worry, frustration, and resentment.

—Dale Carnegie

NANCY WAS *TRULY* in middle management. As a
manager in a retail chain, she often felt caught between
the proverbial rock and a hard place. When customers
were rude, her boss made impossible demands, her employees were late, or a shipment didn't come in on time,
she felt frustrated. In most cases her annoyance would
dissipate of its own accord and she could get back to work.
But over the years, the frustration was having a cumulative effect. She felt anxious, tired, and harried nearly all
the time.

By the time she came to see me, Nancy was like a coiled spring. "What used to roll off me like water off a duck's back is sticking to me," she confessed. "My Teflon is corroding, and I feel close to saying or doing something that I know will be destructive."

As our meetings continued, both she and I began to understand more about not just her frustration, but how frustration operates in general. This understanding crystallized in one session when she realized the source of her unstable emotion.

"When I'm frustrated I feel like a victim—as I do when my boss dumps stuff on me when my plate is full—or I feel self-righteous, as I do when my subordinates make excuses. Once I am fully immersed in my victim mind-set, things quickly deteriorate. I go heads down and make matters worse."

Nancy also noticed that when she left the emotion alone and made some "breathing room," her irritation went away.

> The torment of human frustration, whatever its immediate cause, is the knowledge that the self is in prison, its vital force and "mangled mind" leaking away in lonely, wasteful self-conflict.
>
> —Elizabeth Drew

ON A NEUROLOGICAL LEVEL, what was happening to Nancy—as happens to all of us when we feel the way she does—is that her brain was literally shutting down on her in a "fight or flight" response. Since she felt overwhelmed, her brain went into panic mode, short-circuiting her ability to engage her frontal lobes, the part of the brain that makes higher decisions and modifies impulses.

Nancy was the ideal client because during the course of our sessions she discovered that she had the power to "transform herself" through changing her perspective. Since she was very tactical by nature, she realized that she needed to think differently in order to avoid sliding into her frustrated, seized-up mind-set.

Nancy recognized that she felt like a victim when she felt she had been wronged or that something had been taken away from her. Then she consciously changed her perceptual framework. "I thought about what would happen if I focused on what my company and specifically my boss have *given me*, rather than what they had taken from me," she said.

She came up with three things she felt grateful to her company for: the opportunity to rise to management, the belief that she could handle the job, and her boss's trust and respect. The latter was the tough one but, she said, "I came to see that he respects my ability and capability so much that he doesn't feel he needs to walk on eggshells around me." Her greatest insight came when she realized that she couldn't "be grateful and feel like a victim at the same time."

Nancy's exercise in gratitude allowed her to recenter herself whenever she felt frustrated. It gave her poise when dealing with her boss and graciousness when dealing with her subordinates. In the end, she gained much more respect—not just at work, but from everyone in her life, and for herself.

> One of the sources of pride in being a human being is the ability to bear present frustrations in the interests of longer purposes.
>
> —Helen Merell Lynd

NANCY LEARNED about one of life's little ironies: When you're feeling frustrated, you look for the world to change to make you feel better. Frustration only goes away for good when you change the way you look at the world.

Usable Insight

You can't be grateful and frustrated at the same time.

>>> Action Steps

1. Recognize when you are frustrated as early as you can. Tell yourself, "If I don't do something to make this better, it will only get worse."

2. Counter the possible slide into feeling like a victim by thinking of three things about your job or the person who is frustrating you that you are grateful for.

3. Next time you feel frustrated about something or with someone, pause for as long as you need to until your frustration settles down. Then ask yourself, "Do I just want to get even, or do I want to become more effective at dealing with this situation?"

4. If you find yourself focusing on just getting even, ask yourself, "What will be the short-term and long-term consequences of doing that?" You will probably realize that a negative response just makes matters worse.

Chapter 33

Being
Thin-Skinned

He had a sensation of anxiety and shame, a
sensitivity acute beyond usefulness, as if the
nervous system, flayed of its old hide of
social usage, must record every touch of pain.
—John Updike

JANE HAD A LOT of things going for her—brains,
talent, a loving family, and a good job as a public relations
specialist. She was openhearted, generous, and optimistic,
and people generally liked her.

She was also quite sensitive, which meant that she had
a gift for empathy. She could pick up on other people's
feelings more quickly than most. But her sensitivity cut
both ways and sometimes displayed itself as touchiness. If

she felt she was being slighted or criticized, she would feel very hurt and it took her a long time to recover. When this happened in her family, her spouse or children would spend extra time doing repairs.

Jane generally did well at work, but her sensitivity frequently got in her way. If a colleague wasn't particularly friendly, she wondered what she had done. Performance evaluations were torture for her (see "Fear of Giving or Receiving Performance Reviews"). Her superior would begin by talking about all the good things she had done, but the "need for improvement" comments sent her crashing through the floor. When he pointed out that she had made a mistake or had not been as careful as she needed to be, she would start to cry. After one review, she felt so terrible that she had to leave work for the remainder of the day—leaving her boss to wonder about her mental stability.

It's certainly not unusual to feel badly after being criticized, but people like Jane seem to feel the pricks more sharply than others. If you feel yourself to be thin-skinned—or if others have noted that you seem to be—you no doubt wonder why.

Biologically speaking, skin is a membrane. There are three kinds. An *impermeable* membrane keeps things out. The skin that covers your body is very close to an impermeable membrane; without it you would be prone to infection. Some skin is *semi-permeable,* acting like a filter. The so-called "blood brain" barrier in the human brain lets some substances from the blood in that it needs, such as sugar and oxygen, and keeps others out, such as poisonous toxins. *Permeable* skin allows air, water, and other matter to flow in and out. Bullfrogs, for example, have permeable skin; they absorb water and air through their skin.

As you mature, your psyche has the potential to develop various "skins" of its own. If your psychological experience is imbalanced, you run the risk of becoming either thick-skinned or thin-skinned. When you're thick-skinned (see "Being Closed Off to Input"), you don't let enough in. When you're thin-skinned, you let too much in. You take things and feel things too personally.

> Beauty is only skin deep, and there are millions of people
> in the world that are thin-skinned.
>
> —James Armour

BEING THIN-SKINNED goes hand in hand with being needy. This means that you have your guard down too much of the time and allow too much in. You may hunger for something you didn't get in your youth—unconditional love, support, encouragement, protection from something overwhelming. You need these things as much as you need food or oxygen, and as a result, you've become too permeable. You don't have the boundaries and borders you need to keep bad things out.

Accordingly, you may find yourself in difficult situations, or bringing difficult people into your life, because you don't know how to defend yourself properly. You may be hoping to get something positive, nurturing, affirming, and healing from these situations or people, but you are more likely to get run over or used.

How do you develop a thicker skin? You don't need to become someone you aren't. You can go on being perceptive and empathetic, but you need to develop emotional boundaries, just as good parents set boundaries for their children.

Jane, for example, eventually developed boundaries by thinking of herself as her own good parent. She learned to objectify things more, and check in with herself before and after an unpleasant situation. When such a situation arose, she took time to breathe and calm down before reacting. She prepared for future performance reviews by writing up her own self-critiques and asking a close colleague to go over them with her beforehand, so she would not be surprised by the final verdict.

Jane also learned to adjust her expectations of people around her. She realized that she desperately wanted her boss's approval, just as she had craved the approval of her critical father. When she recognized that she was transferring her feelings about her father to her boss, she realized that she was being unfair to her boss. He was just doing his job the best way he knew how.

By liberating the people around her from the psychological neediness that had driven her, Jane developed better relations with all of them. As a result of this inner work, she became more easygoing and more focused and effective in her work.

Usable Insight

When someone hurts your feelings the first time, shame on them; when they do it a second time, shame on you.

⟫⟫⟫ Action Steps

1. Make a list of situations in which you historically get your feelings hurt, feel disappointed, or become angry.
2. Ask yourself what it is you want and need from the people involved. Then think about what you are likely to receive from them if you ask them.
3. Adjust your expectations to the response you're likely to receive from someone or the result from that situation.

4. Have a backup plan ready in case you receive less than what you expect.

5. Practice setting emotional boundaries by checking in with your emotions and directing yourself to "stop" when you catch yourself taking things too personally.

Chapter 34

Not Learning from Your Mistakes

Man stands in his own shadow and wonders
why it's dark.

—Zen saying

BILL CLINTON HAD TO undergo a near-hanging
before he realized that not admitting to a mistake was a
bad idea. And there are plenty of people—including innumerable politicians—who doggedly go on insisting that
they are in the right, that they have made no mistakes,
that their worldview is unshakable, regardless of the facts.
The problem is that failing to own up to and learn from
mistakes is one of the greatest obstacles to building credi-
bility with and esteem from others.

Why are you unable to admit your mistakes and learn

from them? Almost everyone has trouble admitting mistakes. We feel ashamed that we made them in the first place; when we have to admit to them, we feel ashamed again. We doubt ourselves: If we were wrong about this, we might be wrong about all kinds of things. We fear an explosion of self-doubt. We also fear that we won't be able to learn from the mistake and correct it (see "Fear of Learning New Things").

Ironically, when you fail to own up to your mistakes, the situation becomes worse. This is because the more you deny, the more deeply invested you become in your mistake. You essentially pledge your allegiance to your version of reality, which is in conflict with the other, external one. When your reality comes crashing into the contradictory one, it becomes very hard to admit the difference. So what you do is downplay or justify the mistake, which makes it seem less important than it is.

> Once we realize that imperfect understanding is the
> human condition, there is no shame in being wrong,
> only in failing to correct our mistakes
>
> —George Soros

DOWNPLAYING or justifying your mistake is a way of trying to make a connection between your internal version of reality and that of the outside world. Doing so makes you feel a little better, even if you don't completely escape the embarrassment of getting caught. It temporarily lessens the sting.

How do you escape the vicious cycle? By developing the psychological courage needed to deal with mistakes, it becomes easier to understand that admitting mistakes earns you more respect than it costs you. People who own up to mistakes, and do it in a heartfelt way, are admirable. We look up to those who confront their errors honestly and then make amends. Ironically, the respect you earn from others by admitting and learning from mistakes far outweighs the shame you feel from trying to downplay or justify them. Remember: To err is human; to admit your mistake, classy; to learn from it, divine.

> Life shrinks or expands in proportion to one's courage.
>
> —Anaïs Nin

USABLE INSIGHT

Making a mistake doesn't make you a failure, but failure to admit your mistake might.

⟫⟫⟩ Action Steps

1. Admit mistakes as soon as you can. If you feel defensive about something, that's a hint that it's time to own up to yourself and others.

2. As soon as you recognize the mistake, ask yourself:
   - What do I need to do now to control the damage?
   - What would I have done differently if I had it to do over again?
   - What should I be on the lookout for in the future as the earliest warning sign before I repeat the mistake?

3. Own up to a mistake as soon as possible and share with your boss your answers to the questions above. Your boss will not think less of you and may even think more of you for admitting the mistake. If you come up with solutions for correcting the problem and preventing it from happening again, so much the better.

Chapter 35

Not Getting Buy-In

People buy into the leader before they buy
into the vision.

—John C. Maxwell

TOO OFTEN, the best-laid plans of mice and managers
go nowhere because the managerial mice have skipped the
step of gaining buy-in from the people who will ultimately
execute the managers' plans. When they haven't bought
in, people don't have enough of a stake to sustain their
motivation through the entire length of a project. As soon
as the work becomes too frustrating, they begin to falter,
often with the same justification that adolescents offer
their parents: "It wasn't my idea." In other words, "Don't
expect me to keep trying when things become hard."

Failing to get buy-in sabotages everything, from projects to companies. If you don't get buy-in from teammates, bosses, clients, and others, you won't go anywhere.

One of the most common examples of failure to get buy-in occurs in the world of information technology. Many chief information officers and executives decide to green-light an expensive new IT system that is supposed to rake in more gold from customers (I'm thinking particularly of "customer relationship management" and similar classes of software). The goals are set, the benchmarks created, the testing completed, the rollout rolled out, and then . . . there's the pushback. Employee reaction ranges from threatened and angry to skeptical and passive; they may resent having to learn new things (see "Fear of Learning New Things") or perform previously unrequested tasks. Then management has to force the learning issue, and morale suffers. Happens all the time.

Then there are the personal failures to get buy-in. Chances are you don't buy in to things yourself. How many times has your boss asked you to take on a new assignment and you agreed—not because you wanted to take it on but because he's the boss? You may or may not have done a decent job with the project, but chances are you hardly enjoyed it. And when you put the shoe on the other foot and make demands on someone without getting their complete buy-in, odds are you won't get their best work—if you see any work at all—either.

Not getting buy-in involves a combination of impulses. If you are in a leadership position in which you get to make all the decisions, you probably don't feel like you need it (though you're likely to feel frustrated when you don't get it). That's arrogance—in which case you might want to consider your own fallibility ("Thinking You're Indispensable" can help you with this). Or you may just be so in love with your project that you charge ahead and expect people to be swept right along, in which case you aren't listening ("Not Listening"). Either way, you're getting in the way of your own success.

> To promote cooperation, remember: People tend to resist
> that which is forced upon them. People tend to support
> that which they help to create.
>
> —Vince Pfaff

GETTING BUY-IN first requires the ability to understand the other person's agenda. Very often, your counterpart will have an agenda that stands in direct conflict to what you want. So the first task is to find out what their commitments are, and then to gently sell the other person on your commitments by asking for their involvement. What works is to follow the adage "People try harder at what they *want* to do than at what other people want them to do." In other words, if you want people to participate in moving a project or a company forward, find a way to include them in the decision of how to do it.

> Thee lift me and I lift thee and together we ascend.
>
> —John Greenleaf Whittier

SOMETIMES, the person will nod and make you think you're being understood (for more on this, see "Assuming Others Understand You"). Regardless of the wide range of agendas that people will admit to, there is one underlying agenda that everyone has that you would do well to keep in mind. Whatever you say needs, from their point of view, to: (1) make sense; (2) feel right (that is, not feel shaky); and (3) be doable.

In the absence of a request that makes sense, feels right, and is doable, you create dissonance. "Dissonance" means that what people see and hear doesn't match what they feel. Dissonance usually leads to people opting out. Stated differently, dissonance changes the formula from "What are you going to do *for* me?" to "What are you going to do *to* me?"

On the other hand, when all three things are present, there is a greater chance that people will buy in because what you are saying resonates with them.

USABLE INSIGHT

When something makes sense, feels right, and seems doable, they buy in. When it doesn't, they buy out.

>>> Action Steps

1. Next time you want buy-in from someone or a group of people, make sure that what you say makes sense, feels right, and is doable. You can achieve this by running it by colleagues, friends, and family and asking for their input. In their absence, tape-record and then listen to yourself to see if you'd buy in to what you say.

2. Frequently, something will make sense to the person to whom you are speaking. But it won't feel right or be doable because he or she is already committed to doing something for someone else. In this case, it helps to seek permission from the other person who has a claim on their time.

3. Another way to generate buy-in is to get people to participate in the process of seeing opportunities and overcoming obstacles by asking the following questions:

    ✦ What do you see as the top three opportunities for (*insert the name of your department, work group, or company*)?

    ✦ Do you think these opportunities actually exist (vs. pie-in-the-sky, wishful thinking) and if so, why?

    ✦ What are the top three obstacles that prevent you/us from taking advantage of these opportunities?

    ✦ Most important (and be as specific as possible), who would need to do more of what and stop doing what in order to take advantage of these opportunities?

4. Practice the action steps in "Not Listening." The more heard other people feel, the more likely they are to listen to you.

Chapter 36

Being Devious

Those who think it is permissible to tell
white lies soon grow color-blind.

—Austin O'Malley

ONE OF MY PATIENTS was a man who had been
fired from his job as a sales manager in a technology firm.
Wesley had always been a top salesman, surpassing his
quota quarter after quarter. When a large sale fell through,
it was discovered that Wesley had engaged in what the
industry calls "channel stuffing"—that is, claiming that he
had actually sold products that were still only under consideration at client sites. He had done this not just once
but consistently. When the news of his activities reached

top management, they quietly let him go for fear that his activities would cause the company to run afoul of accounting laws.

Wesley was the fourth of five children. When he was little, he always felt like he lost out on attention: He had to suffer the indignities of hand-me-downs and being talked over at dinner. In the afternoons, before his brothers came home from their after-school sports, he played with their toys. He was very happy doing this, until he broke a toy and his sibling complained to their parents. He was duly reprimanded, and obediently went back to being the quiet, overlooked fourth of five.

Unfortunately, Wesley lived in a household in which he sensed deviousness as "normal" behavior. His father cheated on his mother. On television, he watched stories of people telling lies. His oldest brother thought it was cool to steal from stores. He taught Wesley how to do it: Look nonchalant, make sure no one is around, act fast. Soon Wesley was walking out of stores with loaded pockets. He stole so much that he even gave the stuff away as birthday and Christmas presents. When a store manager caught him and called the police and then his parents, Wesley blamed his brother. Both were duly ashamed and swore they'd never do it again.

> Adults find pleasure in deceiving a child. They consider it necessary, but they also enjoy it. The children very quickly figure it out and then practice deception themselves.
>
> —Elias Canetti

WHEN WESLEY was in college, he had to write term papers. He found Web sites where he could download "A" papers other students had written. He helped himself, and he was never caught. But he admitted that he'd always felt like he had not really earned his final grade, and he was still bothered by this.

Then he went to work in an office and thought nothing of "borrowing" office supplies—pens, Post-its, copy paper—to use at home.

Finally, Wesley became a manager in a big company, and he didn't think much of fudging numbers. "No one will catch it," he thought, "if I just change the spreadsheet date."

One of the dangers of feeling like you can get away with little crimes is that you begin to feel you can get away with bigger ones. Deviousness is like a snowball that sets off an avalanche. You don't have to be a criminal to think like this: corporate leaders obviously think so, too.

When you think you can get away with things, you become entirely focused on yourself. You lose sight of the effects of your actions on other people. Bill Clinton abused his office and his marriage by getting involved with Monica Lewinsky. Clinton had trouble looking into our eyes on television and admitting this, and made it difficult for us to forgive him. (Imagine our different responses if instead he had looked straight out at us and said, "I did wrong in my actions with Monica Lewinsky, I dishonored this office, and worst of all I made it difficult and even embarrassing for you to explain my behavior to your young children.")

Reporters make up sources and stories because they think they will never be questioned. Countless business executives have made a game of robbing shareholders and playing with the accounting rules. Someone at the office works to sabotage a colleague. Why? Because they think they can get away with it. It is fun.

Power confers license. But if you abuse your power to pursue license, you end up betraying a trust—the trust of your siblings, your parents, society, your employer, your public, and, in Clinton's case, your nation. Deviousness generates denial, which generates more deviousness and denial. The whole thing snowballs, and never ends well. Eventually, it all catches up to you.

Deviousness is born from a fundamental feeling of deprivation. That little boy, for example, played with his brothers' toys because he felt he was not getting enough attention and so was justified in taking what he could. So did Shakespeare's Macbeth, who started out as a legitimate lord but was conned into believing he was the rightful king of Scotland. So he killed the king to fast-track his way to the crown. But "murder will out." His wife became so depressed she killed herself, and Macbeth met his end at the hands of his victims' families.

When deviousness is a socially sanctioned habit, it's almost legitimate. Or is it? At what point do your lies get old? How many people do you have to burn before you're tired of burning them? How long can you run on your "luck" before getting caught? And once you are, what do the people you've deceived think? First, they feel hurt—how could you have done that to them? Once the hurt wears off, they begin to hate you for violating their trust. Third, they hesitate to resume a relationship with you.

> If you tell the truth, you never have to remember anything.
>
> —Mark Twain

SURE, it may be fun to feel like you can get away with being devious. But keep it up and you won't have anyone but yourself to blame when your Karma comes calling. But when you understand and embrace the moral truism that "what goes around comes around," you'll live a life you can be proud of.

Usable Insight

People will forgive an honest mistake, but they won't forgive you (or forget) if you lie to them.

⟩⟩⟩ Action Steps

1. *Acknowledge* that you are devious. Deviousness is a habit, an addiction. The first step in recovery is to acknowledge that you have the problem.

2. *Accept* that you have to change your behavior going forward.

3. *Act* henceforth with the understanding that what you put out you get back.

    You must also repair the damage to others by doing the following:

4. Demonstrate *remorse*—acknowledge that your deviousness has caused harm (start by saying, "I hurt you, didn't I?" followed by an acknowledgment that you were wrong. Don't try to *explain* anything —that just makes you look worse).

5. Perform *restitution*—that is, going beyond words to do something to make amends. Clinton did do this, in part by accepting all the negative comments about him and not defending his actions.

6. Demonstrate your *rehabilitation*—to restore trust and faith, you must show others that your behavior has changed for good. Again, Clinton demonstrated his rehabilitation by restoring his relationship with his wife, setting up charitable foundations, and channeling his energies toward productive work.

Chapter 37

Typecasting

After *The Wizard of Oz* I was typecast as a lion,
and there aren't that many parts for lions.

— Bert Lahr

HARRIS, a fifty-six-year-old executive vice president, described to me how he learned a tough lesson about typecasting. Harris ran a division of a large architectural firm and managed a staff of forty people. His assistant, Karen, had worked with him for a month, capably managing his calendar, shielding him from busywork, and competently managing his files. Always anxious to please, Karen tried very hard to earn her boss's rare praise.

But after that month of excellent work, Karen's performance took a nosedive. She began coming in late to work and took frequent sick days. She seemed depressed and unmotivated, and he thought her behavior was becoming erratic. She began making small, and then larger, mistakes. He started assigning various mental labels to her: "Lazy." "Unmotivated." "Screwed-up." "Maybe doing drugs." He thought of his last assistant, who after two years of struggling at her job had revealed her chronic problems with alcohol and drugs.

What Harris really needed was a super-reliable straight arrow—the person Karen had represented herself to be. Now she, too, appeared to be flaking out, like all the others, and sensing the revelation of yet another assistant who lacked character and possibly honesty, Harris found himself becoming curt and disrespectful toward her in return for being bamboozled yet again.

Finally, when Harris missed an important sales meeting, he blew up at her. "You're really messing up lately, Karen," he said. "You'd better start pulling it together, and fast. I can't afford an assistant who isn't performing."

Karen tried to hold back. She shut her eyes and breathed through her nose, but her face began to crumple. Tears started falling.

Her reaction took Harris aback. He felt flummoxed, but he tried to be calm. "Mind telling me what's going on?" he asked.

That's when Karen confessed that her three-year-old son had been diagnosed with leukemia.

When Harris recovered from his shock, he asked softly, "Why didn't you tell me before?"

"It's not something that's easy to talk about," Karen responded. "Besides, you've been very busy and, um . . . a bit grumpy. I didn't feel like it was safe to tell you."

A father himself, Harris obviously felt terrible about misjudging Karen. He immediately put her in touch with the company's human resources manager. He arranged for her to take a leave of absence on half pay, and kept in close touch with Karen and her family through the ordeal. (The boy lost an arm, but eventually recovered, and Karen came back to her job.)

There are deep, primordial psychological reasons for typecasting. First of all, like it or not, we're just built that way. Millions of years of evolution have taught humans to survive dangerous situations by rapidly discerning whether someone from another tribe is friendly or not. Studies have shown that within the first few seconds of laying eyes on a stranger, we've already made firm judgments based solely on their physical traits and behavior. (This is, of course, the root of discrimination.)

This quick-to-judge tendency in humans is exacerbated not just by our demanding jobs, but also by our always-on modern life—tethered as we are to our cell phones, beepers, and computers, not to mention 24/7 news stations warning us of color-coded threats. Because the human brain is incapable of dealing with this "hurry up and respond" information all at once, we live in permanent fight-or-flight survival mode. No wonder we're all so trigger-happy making shoot-first, ask-questions-later judgments.

Second, most of us unconsciously transfer the personal qualities of people we've known in our past—particularly our fathers, mothers, siblings—onto others. We match new people with familiar patterns instead of judging them in their own right. In Harris's case, Karen's "goofing off" reminded him not only of bad experiences with past assistants, but also of his younger brother, who'd rebelled against going to school and fell into trouble with drugs.

Karen, too, unconsciously typecast Harris as a tough father figure whose approval she craved. When her boss became ill-tempered, she shut down and walked on eggshells, as she had done with her own dad. To make matters worse, Harris's and Karen's images of each other reinforced their bad behavior. The grumpier Harris became, the more stressed Karen felt. And the more unfocused Karen became, the grouchier Harris grew. Ironically, they had turned into each other's typecasts.

To succeed, jump as quickly at opportunities
as you do at conclusions.

—Benjamin Franklin

IN WORK situations in which we must trust colleagues, bosses, and employees, typecasting can work against us in several ways. When we're in survival mode—which was the case with Harris—our brains are simply firing "react!" messages too fast, which prevents us from absorbing new information. We become quick-tempered and anxious. We lose our ability to make clear and objective decisions. People are either for us or against us. Likewise, when we typecast on the basis of patterns from our families, we risk falling into behaviors that don't mesh with reality. We make decisions based on emotion rather than on fact. In either case, we eliminate the possibility of doing our best work because we're not really understanding what's going on around us.

I've always found it interesting that people throw away their type-casts at moments of common, physical crisis. After hurricanes, floods, earthquakes, tsunamis, and fires, and in wartime, people come together to help one another survive and recover. It seems that when people are focused on real physical threats from a common opponent, as opposed to the invented threats that live in their heads, they throw prejudice to the wind. How sad that as those common threats that unite us pass, our prejudices return.

USABLE INSIGHT

Jump to conclusions about where people are coming from
and they'll resist going where you want them to go.

>>> Action Steps

1. Think of an instance when you were typecast without the other person's really understanding you. Remember how hurt, angry, and frustrated you were. Would you want to make someone feel the way you felt?

2. Think of a colleague whom you negatively stereotype and come up with three one-word labels for that person. Next time you're together, ask yourself whether you're listening to the labels or to your colleague. If you find yourself listening or speaking in a way that bears out the labels, ask yourself whether you could be wrong.

3. Resist the impulse to see people as functions rather than as people with talents and skills. Don't assume that because someone is lower on the totem pole than you are that they deserve less than gracious attention.

4. When working on a project or problem together, focus on the issue or task, not on the person.

5. Check out your assumptions before acting on them.

Chapter 38

Setting Your Expectations Too Low

> Our limitations and success will be based,
> most often, on our own expectations for
> ourselves. What the mind dwells upon,
> the body acts upon.
>
> —Dennis Waitley

ONCE UPON A TIME there was a little boy named Mark (yours truly) who read a comic book in the backseat of the family car, got carsick, and threw up. From that moment on, his mother told him that he must not read in the car or he would become carsick. And voilà—every time he read in the car he got sick. He could read on planes and trains, because his mother never warned him about them.

Some forty years later, I was driving with my wife to San Diego. I had just bought a book I wanted to read, and since she was at the wheel, I was determined once and for all to stop missing out on the opportunity to catch up on reading on the many occasions when she was driving. So I brought along a vomit bag and told myself I was going to read that magazine, even if I threw up for the entire drive.

I began reading. Three minutes into the trip, I felt nauseated. But eventually the queasiness passed. And I have been able to read in a car ever since. The mind is an amazing thing, isn't it?

Most of us live comfortably within a box of limitations. We "know" we are good at some things and not at others. We "know" we're lousy at accounting or writing. So we choose work and tasks that fit within our limitations, never dreaming that we are capable of much more.

Most people don't achieve what they can because they have preset low expectations of themselves. The reasons spring from low self-confidence, pessimism, or possibly even clinical depression. They may also spring from the notion of "learned helplessness" (see "Quitting Too Soon"), which tells you that some things are just not worth the effort. You may believe that if you attempt something new and it doesn't work out, you'll just be disappointed—so why should you try at all?

Low expectations usually spring from a fundamental belief that some things are just impossible or that you won't be able to handle the repercussions if you fail to meet higher ones. Both of these often date back to childhood, when your parents either discouraged you from setting expectations too high or pushed you to set them so high that you set yourself up to fail. The key is that in either case your disappointment did not elicit the comfort and coaching that would have built resilience in you.

When you set low expectations, you're stuck in "yes, but" consciousness. You agree that you would like to live larger, but. . . . But. But.

Once you say you're going to settle for second,
that's what happens to you in life.

—John F. Kennedy

WHAT ABOUT so-called "stretch goals"? Aren't they designed to help you achieve more? At work, your boss may ask you to do more or tackle projects that he or she may feel you can handle that require more responsibility or coordination than what you are currently doing. Unfortunately, stretch goals don't really stretch you as much as they apply more pressure, because your boss may merely be asking you to do more of the same, though possibly on a slightly larger playing field. Your imagination may remain boxed in. And that's too bad.

A true "stretch goal" is something that springs from within—an internal desire to be or do something you aren't yet being or doing. When you can tap into that inner vision, it's amazing to see what you are capable of.

Not long ago, I spoke with Leonard Kleinrock, a professor of computer science at UCLA. Dr Kleinrock created the basic principles of packet switching, which is the underpinning technology of the Internet, while he was a student at MIT—ten years *before* the birth of the Internet. In 1999, the *Los Angeles Times* listed him as one of the fifty people who had most influenced business in the twentieth century. Here's a fellow who knows a lot about stretch goals. Here's what he told me:

"With all due modesty, much has been written about my accomplishments, prizes, and awards. But if you were to look at the framed collage of awards, prizes, and degrees that is displayed in my home, you will notice that smack dead center in the middle is the one that means the most to me and the source of the best advice I received and followed. It's my Eagle Scout award."

High expectations are the key to everything.

—Sam Walton

"WHEN HE WAS A CHILD growing up in Manhattan, one of the things Dr. Kleinrock loved was being a Boy Scout. "I worked hard to rise in the ranks," he recalled, "and when I reached the level of Star Scout, my scoutmaster, Mr. Spinner, told me, 'Len, if you really work at it, I believe you can become the first Eagle Scout this troop has ever had.' That was a real challenge—one seemingly out of reach for a city-bound kid living in Manhattan, far away from the woods. But I took the challenge, set my mind and body to it, and in 1951, I did indeed become the troop's first Eagle Scout."

Don't lower your expectations to meet your performance. Raise your level of performance to meet your expectations. Expect the best of yourself, and then do what is necessary to make it a reality.

—Ralph Marston

THAT CHALLENGE has directed much of the way Dr. Kleinrock has lived his life. It told him that by selecting a goal for himself that seemed out of reach, and then working very hard, the goal was in fact achievable. And one goal leads to another, for once you cross one hurdle that you thought was impossible, the other hurdles don't seem so high after all. "And when you discover you can do that, it empowers you to keep stretching yourself into worlds and wonders that you might never think of reaching for, and succeeding at them," Dr. Kleinrock told me. "It's all about not giving up if you want something badly enough."

⟫⟫⟫ Action Steps

Overcoming Your Fear of Disappointment

1. Think of three times in your career when you had high expectations that didn't pan out.

2. How long did it take to get over each one?

3. What did you do to get over them?

4. What would be the best thing to do to get over them?

5. Make a commitment to doing that when you set expectations that don't come through.

Setting Stretch Goals

6. Ask yourself the Impossibility Question (developed by consultant Dave Hibbard of Profit Techniques in Irvine, California): "What would be impossible to do, that if you could do it, would dramatically accelerate your results and your career?" By answering this question up front, you bypass your "Yes, but" response.

7. What would be a strategy to make your impossible dream possible?

8. What's the first step in that strategy?

9. Now take that first step. (And don't drop the ball by adjusting the goal to make it smaller and more limited. Just keep plugging away.)

Chapter 39

Assuming Others Understand You

The greatest problem in communication is
the illusion that it has been accomplished.
—George Bernard Shaw

TOM WAS what you might call an "idea man." A creative
senior communications manager in a mid-sized company,
Tom had been promoted to oversee a staff of six people.
Every so often, Tom would invite one of his staff members
to brainstorm one of his ideas with him, and then assign
the individual to follow up.

The staff loved Tom, and they liked his ideas—or at
least wanted to believe they did. But Tom had a mind that
raced ahead of him, and he—like most managers—had
too much on his plate. Very often a staffer would return

with what was supposed to be a "completed assignment." But Tom would discover that the staffer had gone off in a completely different direction than the one he thought they had discussed.

This frustrated everyone, of course. Most of all it frustrated Tom, who thought he had clearly delegated the task. It also ate up more of Tom's time to go back and retrack; sometimes he decided to do the work himself, with the result that he had less time than ever.

Eventually, Tom burned out and asked to be removed from management. He took a cut in salary, but he was glad to be relieved of the responsibility of directing other people. Assuming that his staffers understood him interfered with his interpersonal effectiveness. He thought he was a good communicator, but he didn't become aware of the problem until he was out of commission.

Why do you assume people understand you when they don't? One reason is that, on a neuroanatomical level, your brain, like Tom's, may not be able to tell what's coming from what's going. Your posterior nervous system (from the posterior side of your spinal cord up into your posterior cortex) is focused on sensory input. That means it's receiving input from the world, including what people say to you. Your anterior nervous system (from your anterior spinal cord up to your cranial nerves and frontal cortex) is focused on motor function. That means it's focused on outward expression—what you say or do out toward the world.

Simply put, what you take in and think and what you communicate to others come from two entirely different regions of your brain. When something is very clear in your mind, you may tend to assume that you are communicating clearly to another person when in fact you are not. The two regions of your brain become connected only when you ask others if they understand what you are saying.

When I worked with stroke patients, the issue of effective communication was always brought home to me. The most common language-related strokes result in a brain injury that produces aphasia—the partial or total loss of the ability to verbally communicate ideas or comprehend spoken or written language. The tragedy of aphasia is that patients understand much more than they can communicate.

In so-called Wernicke's (posterior sensory) aphasia, the damage occurs in a posterior part of the cortex, which causes patients to not understand what they hear. Their anterior (motor) cortex is spared so they can speak fluently, but because they lack understanding or comprehension, they don't make any sense to anyone.

In Broca's (anterior motor) aphasia, patients understand what is said to them, because their posterior (sensory) cortex, which governs the ability to comprehend, is spared. Yet their damaged anterior cortex makes it difficult for them to communicate what they understand.

People like Tom, who think they are getting through when they aren't, remind me of patients with Wernicke's aphasia. By this I mean that they don't realize when others are not understanding them. They just continue to speak fluently in a way that doesn't make any sense to those they are talking to. Fortunately for people like Tom, the analogy here is just an analogy. Unlike such stroke patients who are neurologically unable to comprehend, Tom needs to focus on really understanding the people with whom he is communicating, so that both he and they know that what he says to them gets through.

The problem of assuming people understand you is compounded when you have authority over the person you're speaking to. Such a person may not be comfortable asking for clarification. This is what caused problems for Tom.

When we issue instructions to people, we rarely ask for confirmation beyond a vague nod and "uh-huh." Consider what happened during the O. J. Simpson criminal trial, in which I served as an adviser to the prosecution (see "Using Jargon"). At the end of the long trial, Judge Ito gave the jury jargon-free but lengthy and detailed instructions. After every few instructions, he would ask the jury, "Do you understand?" after which the group would dutifully nod. As he continued, it became clear to nearly everyone in the courtroom that the jury may have heard what Judge Ito was saying but they did not understand.

The question "Do you understand?" does not guarantee understanding. Moreover, it infantilizes the person you are speaking to. No wonder people really understand so little, despite appearances.

Interpersonal communication gets even more complicated when you try to force understanding down the other person's throat—that is, when you keep elaborating or persisting in giving too many examples of what you are trying to say. When this happens, the other person, who may, in fact, understand you perfectly well, becomes impatient. This can cause your listener to resent you and then react by *not wanting* to understand you because you've belabored the subject.

> Many attempts to communicate are nullified by saying too much.
>
> —Robert Greenleaf

IF YOU assume people understand you when they don't, you fortunately have a distinct advantage over real stroke patients. In order to correct this problem, all you have to do is ask the other person to repeat what they understand back to you. Judge Ito might have evoked a clearer, more visceral understanding of his instructions had he asked them, "What do you understand about what I have instructed you to do?"

> Asking the right questions takes as much skill as giving the right answers.
>
> —Robert Half

>>> **Action Steps**

1. Check in with your listeners by saying to them, "I'm not sure I've been clear. What do you understand about what I've said?" Practice this on family or close friends first until you get the right tone; then do it at work.

2. Tape-record yourself as often as you can. You can even do this while making phone calls. (People say they don't like to do this because they don't like the sound of their voice, but the fact is it's the tone they dislike.) Listen for instances when you're not communicating clearly or you're whining or pontificating and so on. Again, think about asking a family member or a close friend to listen with you. There's good news and bad news about taping yourself and listening. The bad news is you *will* probably dislike what you hear; the good news is that you will improve how well others understand you.

Chapter 40

Fear of
Failing

No matter how hard you work for success, if
your thought is saturated with the fear of
failure, it will kill your efforts, neutralize
your endeavors, and make success
impossible.

—Baudjuin

"MY FATHER WORKED FOR a company that went
through a major management upheaval. Everyone but
my dad got fired," Steven Sample told the future leaders
attending "The Art and Adventure of Leadership," the
course he teaches with leadership guru and colleague
Warren Bennis at the University of Southern California.
Sample is president of the university, and is credited not

merely with the school's ascendance in sports, but more important also with its ascent to the level of respect as an educational institution that is now one of the most selective in the country.

"My dad went on to tell me that *not* getting fired was the worst thing that ever happened to him in his career," Sample continued. "The other people who had been cut loose from this management-challenged company grew and thrived wherever they landed. My dad remained stuck. It stunted his professional growth and reduced his ultimate satisfaction in his career. He wanted to prevent the same thing from happening to me." Sample was passing on his father's better-late-than-never advice about the positive aspects of failure.

> Failure seldom stops you, what stops you is fear of failure.
>
> —Jack Lemmon

WHAT IS it about failure that is so frightening to people? Is it the rejection? The humiliation? The blow to one's confidence and ego? Or is it simply not being able to take a punch when the failure hits?

Much of it goes back to how your childhood failures were rewsponded to (see "Self-Defeat: What Goes In, Comes Out" in the introduction, and appendix 1). If you were *coddled, criticized,* or *ignored* after a mistake, this added insult to the injury that messing up had already caused you. (Even coddling sooner or later becomes a negative, as you are told that you are "spoiled" by the parents who spoiled you.) If instead you were given the combination of comfort and guidance that *supportive* parents, teachers, or relatives provide, mistakes and failures would be the lessons you have yet to learn rather than wounds to your psyche.

Sample went on to describe how a major failure in his life directly contributed to his greatest success. In 1990 he was a candidate to become president of Ohio State University. He was told by the trustees that he was clearly the front runner and in all probability would be offered the job in a day or two. Sample believed the job was his.

After his interview, which Sample believed was simply a formality, he flew from Columbus, Ohio, on a private jet for a vacation with his family. The next day he received a message that the trustees had changed their minds, and that the job had been offered to someone else.

That may have been considered a failure, according to Sample, but had he become president of Ohio State, he would have never become president of USC (as he did in 1991) and would never have had the opportunity to lead one of the greatest turnarounds in academic excellence in the history of American higher education.

The way to succeed is to double your failure rate.

—Thomas Watson

USABLE INSIGHT

It's not the fear of failure that stops you, but the fear of not being able to handle your reaction when it happens.

>>> Action Steps

1. When faced with something you're afraid to do, ask yourself: "What's the worst thing that will happen if I fail?" Then ask yourself: "What's the worst thing that will happen if I don't

even try?" You will personally experience this: People regret more what they didn't do than what they did.

2. The next time you fail, say to yourself (as often as necessary): "Let time pass, and don't do anything to make things worse." This will prevent you from sliding into a self-defeating behavior that adds embarrassment to the situation and distracts you from learning the lessons a mishap can teach you.

3. Resist the temptation to blame others, to beat up on yourself, or to make excuses.

4. Reach out to supportive people and ask them, "Have you ever done something so stupid that you have trouble accepting that you did it?" or "Have you ever felt that as certain as you thought you were was as wrong as you turned out to be?" Then get ready for the outpouring of commiseration and in many cases a deepening of relationships.

Epilogue

Succeeding in Life as Well as at Work

> It's easy to make a buck. It's a lot tougher
> to make a difference.
>
> —Tom Brokaw

THIS BOOK FOCUSES ON helping you get out of your own way so you can be more successful on the job. Though failing in your career usually results in unhappiness, success doesn't guarantee happiness. Because of my roots as a "healer," I would be remiss in writing a book that helps you succeed at work if it doesn't also help you succeed at life.

Seven years ago I made a house call to an extremely successful and wealthy entertainment industry icon who was dying from liver failure. Jeff had drunk with apparent impunity for the majority of his sixty-three years, but his behavior had finally caught up to him. Choosing to die at home, he was severely withdrawing into himself. According to his doctors, at the time he called me he had only a month to live.

Jeff looked terrible, and I told him so. "I don't think you look this bad just because you're dying," I said bluntly. "You've been dying as long as I've known you." I think Jeff appreciated my directness because, in battling such a bold foe as cirrhosis, the last thing he wanted around him were people who were too timid or, worse, sycophantic.

He stared at me for a minute. Then he looked down at the floor. After a pause he said, "I don't think I've ever done anything important in my life."

"You're crazy!" I replied. "You started an entire industry. You created thousands of jobs. You brought entertainment to millions. You earned boatloads of awards. And you've achieved more than anyone I know."

"Oh, stop the bullshit," Jeff said sharply. "I don't want to hear it. Don't con a con man, especially when he's dying."

He was silent for a minute. "I have all the adoration that money can buy. I have a mansion in Beverly Hills, a château in southern France, and a house at Lake Tahoe. I have a hundred million in assets. I also have two ex-wives. My kids are neurotic failures who can't think for themselves because I was so busy having to be right. Right now after seeing the body count of people I have throttled in my life, I'm thinking that I always won the battles, but have lost the war when it comes to a life that was worth living."

It was as if Citizen Kane had finally confessed. I admired Jeff's courage in admitting what a wreck he'd made of his personal life, though the recognition was sad indeed.

Jeff died four years before the horrors of September 11, 2001. After 9/11, people in my profession saw a sharp rise in the number of depressed and anxious patients who wondered, as Jeff did, what their lives were really good for. On a national level, people from every stratum of society began searching for meaning—spending more time with their families and at church and synagogue, and looking for a sense of mission in their work.

There was another equal and opposite effect of the tragedy. President George Bush urged us to live our lives as usual, to take vacations and go shopping. As housing prices continuously rose, a huge proportion of people took out equity loans and second mortgages on their homes. It was as if we'd all been diagnosed with a terminal disease and had a month to live. We decided that we'd better get out there and run up the credit cards before the end came.

The disconnect between spiritual hunger and rampant consumerism showed up in my practice, of course. I began to see more and more wealthy and successful people who were achievement machines on a financial level, but who were not able to achieve true fulfillment or happiness.

The endless drumbeat of media advertising tells us that the more money you have and spend, the happier you will be. Jeff fell for that philosophy hook, line, and sinker. The old ethic of "keeping up with the Joneses" remained alive and well for him and most Americans. But even as we spent our money to keep up by buying BMWs, bangles, and big backyard barbeques, we found ourselves trying ever harder to keep up with our spiraling debt. As Jeff found out, having all the toys in the world doesn't necessarily mean you win in the end.

You don't have to be dying (like Jeff) or to have barely escaped a terrorist attack to realize that what's most important in your life has nothing to do with possessions.

What's the subject of life—to get rich? All of those
fellows out there getting rich could be dancing around
the real subject of life.

—Paul A. Volcker

SOME YEARS AGO, famed special effects master Stan Winston
shared what made his life worth living. I was attending a board meeting
of a charitable organization, Free Arts for Abused Children, that was
being held in Stan's amazing studio in Van Nuys, California. (Stan was
the charity's greatest financial supporter. He had donated some of his
creations—Arnold Schwarzenegger's *Terminator* head and *Jurassic Park*'s
velociraptor model—for silent auction at the charity's fundraisers.)

The board members were seated around a central table when the
chairman said, "I think we should all show our appreciation to Stan
Winston, who has for several years been our angel."

Stan had been sitting on the periphery. After the applause of appreciation by the board members, Stan blushed and said, "No, no. You have
it all backwards. This charity is *my* angel. I have been blessed in being
able to make a great living doing what I love to do, but I don't really
know how much I help the world by entertaining people. This charity
helps me to know that I *am* making the world a better place. *You* are my
angel and conscience. I am the one that should be grateful to *you*."

Only a life lived for others is worth living.

—Albert Einstein

▶▶▶ Action Steps

1. Make a list of things that were important to focus on and accomplish immediately after September 11. Do the same for things that you thought were unimportant.

2. Elicit from a "sponsor" (your spouse, a close friend, a family member, or someone you highly respect) what they discovered after September 11, and write that down.

3. Think before you shop. Next time you think about dropping $100 for something you don't really need, send that money to a charity instead.

4. Tell your sponsors that you would like them to hold you accountable and in return you will hold them accountable to take actions consistently over time that reinforce the higher humanitarian goals of your life.

5. Set times when you will check in with one another to make sure you are both following through.

6. Every day say thank you for something to someone—perhaps to one of those faceless people who park cars, work as supermarket cashiers, or try to answer your technical questions on the phone to fix something. Try to touch the human being inside the function they're providing. It'll lift them up. . . . It will lift *you* up.

Appendix 1

Where Self-Defeating Behavior Starts

2 STEPS FORWARD, 1 STEP BACK

Birth ›› First breath

Awake ›› Sleep through night

Crawling ›› First step

Stay at home ›› First day of preschool

Elementary school ›› Middle school

Middle school ›› High school

High school ›› College

College ›› Career, marriage

Life ›› Death

Home, Sweet Home — SEPARATION ANXIETY — ← RAPPROCHEMENT — PRACTICING → — INDIVIDUATION ANXIETY — World Is Your Oyster

© 2005 Mark Goulston, M.D.

Appendix 2

How Self-Defeating Behavior Develops

2 Steps Forward, 3 Steps Back

Childhood Challenge
1st Step Forward (= Superbaby)
2nd Step Forward Then You Fall (= Powerless baby)
Rapprochement (= Looking Back)

Your Parent's Reaction			
Coddling	Critical	Ignoring	Supportive

Your Response			
Tantrums	Hurt/Anger	Fear	Confidence

Your Adolescent Thinking			
("Do it for me")	("I'll show you!")	("It'll never work")	("I can do it")

Your Adolescent Attitude			
Spoiled	Hostile	Defeatist	Motivated

Adulthood Obstacle			
Your Adult Reaction			
SELF-DEFEATING BEHAVIOR			*SUCCESSFUL BEHAVIOR*
Compulsions	Blaming	Avoidance	Determination

Your Adult Life			
Lost	Bitter	Empty	Satisfied

Your Life			
W A S T E D			FULFILLED

Twelve Steps to Getting Out of Your Own Way at Work

1. Read through the table of contents and list the self-defeating behaviors with which you most identify.

2. Add to the list any other behaviors that you think may be applicable, or that aren't listed in the book.

3. Ask trusted friends, family members, or colleagues (your "stakeholders") to go through the table of contents and identify self-defeating behaviors they believe are a problem for you.

4. Ask them to add other behaviors that aren't in the book.

5. Rate to what degree you engage in these self-defeating behaviors on a scale of 1 to 3 (where 1 = very little; 2 = somewhat; 3 = frequently).

6. Have your stakeholders rate the degree to which they observe you engaging in self-defeating behaviors according to the scale in step 5.

7. Once you've collected the responses, rank the self-defeating behaviors in order of importance. (Hint: The most important will be the behavior that causes others to lose the most trust

and confidence in you or respect for you, and conversely, the one that if corrected will most rapidly help you regain them.)

8. Select the top two or three most self-defeating behaviors you want to overcome and read the pertinent chapters in this book.

9. As you progress, ask your stakeholders' permission to contact them every month to see what they notice with regard to your behavior.

10. Persevere. Remember, it takes a month for a change in behavior to become a habit, and a minimum of six months to a year for a habit to become part of your personality.

11. After you have overcome your first two self-defeating behaviors, repeat steps 1 through 9 above.

12. Once you have *practiced* the approach above and seen it work (i.e., succeed), you are in a position to *preach* it and assist your people in getting out of their own way.

Appendix 4

The Self-Other
Inventory

This tool helps you evaluate people for a performance review; it also lessens the stress of doing one by helping to make explicit, realistic expectations for your people. You can use it to discuss your observations and ask the employee how he or she might see things differently. It also logically leads to areas of needed improvement.

THE SELF-OTHER INVENTORY

	What I can rely on you for	*What I can't rely on you for*	*What you can rely on me for*	*What you can't rely on me for*
COMPETENCE	To do your job without making significant errors	To get all the details correct	To tolerate a problem as long as it doesn't adversely affect the end result and/or the work of other people	To tolerate a problem if it adversely affects the end result or someone eles's work
ACCOUNT-ABILITY				

	What I can rely on you for	What I can't rely on you for	What you can rely on me for	What you can't rely on me for
INITIATIVE				
SELF-RELIANCE				
TEAM PLAYING				
INTEGRITY				
ATTITUDE				
LOYALTY				

Acknowledgments

ALL BOOKS, nonfiction and fiction, are a collaborative effort. Sometimes the collaborators are explicit—they are actual people who help you in the process of writing a book. At other times they're implicit—they are people who have influenced you and inspired you to write the book.

In my case, the list of explicit and implicit contributors is lengthy. I live near Hollywood, where brevity is encouraged in giving thanks at the Oscar® and Emmy award ceremonies. Even so, I feel compelled to fully acknowledge those people without whom this book would not have been written.

At the top of the list is my recently departed and dearly appreciated mentor, Albert Dorskind, whose common sense and centering guidance over the past twenty years have enabled me to minimize the amount of time I have spent *getting in my own way.* Strong in his opinions but not opinionated, Al talked *to* and *with* me rather than *over* and *at* me, as I have tried to do with you, my readers.

A close second is Ken Florence, another person who has passed on and left a hole in my life. Ken was a top-notch labor attorney and the first business leader to see the relevance and value of my clinical experience to the corporate world. I will forever be grateful for his encouragement, especially during times when I had significant doubts. I still hear him saying, "Mark, everyone out here gets in their own way!"—delivered with his characteristic upbeat laugh.

A not-too-distant third—and mercifully, living—person on my list is my Putnam editor, John Duff, whose persevering confidence and belief in my earlier effort, *Get Out of Your Own Way,* encouraged me to write this book to parallel my journey from my clinical practice of psychotherapy into the world at large. The clarity and succinctness of this volume is owed to John's direct, deft yet sensitive input. I'm also very grateful to my friend B., who helped me beyond description in preparing this book for publication.

Thanks to my wonderful and ever-busy agent, Loretta Barrett, who was never too busy to take my calls, for her enthusiasm and keeping me on track with this project when I would keep throwing ideas at her for subsequent books. Even now, I can hear her telling me, "Focus, Mark! Every season has its purpose. Don't turn, turn, turn."

I am also indebted to Philip Goldberg, my coauthor on *Get Out of Your Own Way,* who developed the format that has served as such a great structure and template that I was able to forge ahead and write this one on my own. I'm grateful, too, to my former agent, Lynn Franklin. Lynn was instrumental in the earlier part of my career; she cemented my relationship with Putnam and was responsible for the extensive foreign publications of my books.

Thanks also to John Byrne and Heath Row, who have given me an opportunity to reach the business public through my "Leading Edge" columns at *Fast Company* magazine; to Deborah Davidson, editor in chief of publications at National Association of Corporate Directors, who has enabled me to connect with American business leaders through my "Directions" columns; to Larry Gerber and Gail Polevoi, who did the same at *Emmy* magazine; to Professionals Network Group for giving me the equivalent of an MBA without having to go to school; to Martin Pichinson, Michael Maidy, and Harry Glazer at Sherwood Partners for a platform for my multiple services; and to Wendy Johnson, founder of the Worldwide Association of Business Coaches, for a place to work with business leaders.

During the course of this project it has been my good fortune to speak with a number of luminaries in the business world, *some* of whom have been included in anecdotes in this book, *all* of whom have influenced the concepts, insights, and action steps. These include: Marjorie Abrams, Madelyn Alfano, Walter Anderson, Dana Ardi, Rosanne Badowski, Barbara Ballinger, Stan Barkey, Tony Baxter, Warren Bennis, Jeffrey Berg, Jordan Bender, Gordon Binder, Charlene Bleakley, David Booth, Paddy Calistro, Lee Canter, George Coelho, Christopher Coffey, Dick Dadamo, Marie Deary, Kathy Doheny, Walter Dunn, Bob Eckert, Anne Fisher, Don Franco, Miriam Friedman, the late Peter Frost, Bronwyn Fryer, Dave Fuller, Larry Gerber, Gene Goda, Marshall Goldsmith, Sidney Harman, Michael Heisley, Patrick Henry, Dave and Marhnelle Hibbard, Rory Hume, Carol Hymowitz, Ron Inge, Brian Katz, Jim Kennedy, Jeffrey Kichaven, Leonard Kleinrock, Mark Lefko, Patrick Lencioni, Mike Leven, Chris Lewis, Chris Mallburg, Jim Mazzo, Thomas McLain, Stacy Robin Meranus, Steve Mindell, Jonathan Murray, Debra Myerson, Barbara Oberman, Billy Pittard, Christopher Platt, Rick Rhoads, Mark Risley, Terri Robinson, Judy Rosener, Lee Ryan, Steven Sample, Jonathan Seybold, Deborah Shames, Bob Sinnott, Rosa Sinnott, Kevin Sharer, Edwin Shneidman, Tom Stewart, Linda Stone, Larry Thomas, A. Raymond Tye, John Tyson, Linda Valentine, Kate White, Bruce Wright, and Richard Saul Wurman.

A man without family is a man without a home. I am truly blessed to have had the support of my wife, Lisa, and children Lauren, Emily, and Billy—ever felt, every step of the way, albeit delivered with a teasing style that loving families often show. Beyond them, the support of my brothers and their wives, Noel and Mary, and Robert and Angela, has been significant. Then there is my mother, Ruth Goulston, still going strong at an age I won't mention and a model of perseverance for me. And of course the memory of my father *and* dad, Irving Goulston, who has been gone more than ten years. It seems he passed on yesterday.

On a final note, I do not believe this book would or could have been written, were it not for the continuing contributions and trust of the patients from my clinical practice, the clients from my consulting practice, and the readers of my books, articles, and columns.

Thanks, everyone.